Boy Soldier of the Confederacy

Boy Soldier
of the
Confederacy

The Memoir of
Johnnie Wickersham

Edited by Kathleen Gorman

Southern Illinois University Press / Carbondale

Copyright © 1918 by John R. Wickersham
Introduction, notes, and bibliography copyright © 2006 by the
Board of Trustees, Southern Illinois University
All rights reserved
Printed in the United States of America
09 08 07 06   4 3 2 1

Library of Congress Cataloging-in-Publication Data
Wickersham, John T., 1846–1916.
    [Gray and the blue]
    Boy soldier of the Confederacy : the memoir of Johnnie
Wickersham / edited by Kathleen Gorman.
        p. cm.
Originally published under title: The gray and the blue. Berkeley,
Calif. : J.T. Wickersham, 1915.
Includes bibliographical references and index.
    1. Wickersham, John T., 1846–1916. 2. United States—History—Civil
War, 1861–1865—Personal narratives, Confederate. 3. Confederate States
of America. Army. Missouri Infantry Regiment, 1st. 4. Missouri—
History—Civil War, 1861–1865—Personal narratives. 5. Missouri—
History—Civil War, 1861–1865—Regimental histories. 6. United
States—History—Civil War, 1861–1865—Regimental histories.
7. United States—History—Civil War, 1861–1865—Participation,
Juvenile. 8. Soldiers—Missouri—Biography. 9. Child soldiers—
Missouri—Biography. I. Gorman, Kathleen, date. II. Title.
E569.51st .W53 2006
973.7'82092—dc22
ISBN-13: 978-0-8093-2722-5 (cloth : alk. paper)
ISBN-10: 0-8093-2722-8 (cloth : alk. paper)   2006003983

Printed on recycled paper. ♻

The paper used in this publication meets the minimum requirements of
American National Standard for Information Sciences—Permanence of
Paper for Printed Library Materials, ANSI Z39.48-1992. ♾

Contents

Acknowledgments

This work would not have been possible without Becky Pierce, who generously shared Johnnie Wickersham's memoir with me and allowed me to work with it. A faculty research grant from Minnesota State University (MSU), Mankato, provided funding and invaluable research assistance. A teaching scholar fellowship from MSU also was instrumental in allowing me to finish this work.

The geography department at MSU Mankato created the map. Cindy Miller was of special assistance.

Providing great help was Beth Luey, who is probably shocked that I remember anything from her classes at Arizona State University. Jan Walmsley assisted me throughout the project. Lynndee Kemmet was essential in editing and reorganizing. Jim Wheaton was a great graduate assistant, whose knowledge was invaluable. Thanks also to Sylvia Rodrigue and Wayne Larsen.

My colleagues in the history department provided expertise and humor in helping me finish this book. Special thanks to Charles Piehl for reading and commenting. Also thanks to my mom for her support.

Introduction

It is not uncommon for men of war to embellish their wartime exploits to the point of myth, and Johnnie Wickersham was no exception. In 1915, at the age of sixty-nine, Wickersham put to paper the stories of his Civil War years that had entertained his family for decades. Throughout his writings, fact mingles with fiction, the line separating the two often difficult to determine. It would thus be easy to dismiss Wickersham's remembrances as useless for historical study. But both fact and fiction are valuable—the fact for what it tells us of the Civil War experience for the average young Confederate, the fiction for what it says of the need for veterans on a losing side to maintain the honor of their cause.[1]

The primary way for the South (and its veterans) to honor its cause was through the development of the "Lost Cause," a theory propagated by Edward Pollard beginning in 1866 that sought both to explain the unexplainable, the South's defeat, and to unify the defeated region. Proponents of the Lost Cause transformed the Civil War itself from a violent, bloody affair into a holy crusade. The onus for the loss was carefully and deliberately shifted from the soldiers to something neither they nor the region could control, the resources of their enemy. This shift transformed those who fought the war from mere men into mythical heroes.[2] Wickersham probably never knew anything about the Lost Cause or Edward Pollard. However, his story illustrates the ideas of the Lost Cause quite well. Wickersham's Confederate comrades are unfailingly brave and moral and good. In the one case in which he shows a Confederate soldier to be less than perfect, the soldier is killed by a truer Southerner. It is stories like Wickersham's that provided support for the myths of the Lost Cause and the Old South.

Veterans wrote their memoirs not only to record their memories but also to influence the way the next generation of Southerners learned about their cause and their history. They wanted to ensure that no one would forget what they had done and why they had done it. Veterans of the Civil War worried that their sons and grandsons would misunderstand—or worse, forget—the struggles of their elders. While individual veterans might write their stories for a small audience (as Wickersham wrote his for his family), some supporters of the Confederate cause had bigger goals in mind. And the memoirs of Southern veterans would figure into these goals.

It is in the Southern veterans' organizations that one finds evidence for this larger cause. Unlike their Northern counterparts, Southern groups tended to be more splintered than the North's powerful Grand Army of the Republic. It was not until 1889 that the United Confederate Veterans (UCV) was founded in the South. An even more long-lasting organization was founded in 1895, when the United Daughters of the Confederacy (UDC) began operation. Article 2 of the UDC constitution makes the purpose of this organization clear: "to instruct and instill into the descendants of the people of the South a proper respect for the pride in the glorious war history." The UDC was obviously more interested in creating and maintaining the glorious myth than in providing any kind of objective history. Many of the most lasting monuments and memorials to Confederate veterans were created by the UDC, not the UCV. Even the crosses on veterans' graves were placed there by the UDC.[3]

The creation and activity of the UDC had to have been well known to Johnnie. The first "Daughters of the Confederacy" was organized in St. Louis in 1890. When the group held fund-raisers throughout the state to build a home for disabled Confederate veterans, they took in twenty-five thousand dollars, accomplishing what a previous Confederate veteran's organization in the state had been unable to do. The Missouri chapter of the UDC was also one of the first in the nation to focus on education, establishing an education committee even before the national group did.[4] It is highly unlikely that a Confederate veteran (such as Johnnie or his brothers) living in Missouri in the decades after the war could have avoided the reach or the viewpoint of the UDC.

Honoring the men who fought the war continued long after the war itself was over. Any major Civil War battlefield is literally covered with monuments that trace the movements of each regiment. These monuments are not only on battlefields but everywhere from county parks to cemeteries. It is a rare Southern county that does not have at least one memorial to the Confederate soldier. Not only was the public constantly reminded of the sacrifices of veterans, but the veterans themselves were continually reminded of the war and their ongoing duties to the public. Just by walking into a county building, a veteran was forcibly reminded of his past and of what the public thought he was. It is easy to imagine Wickersham walking into the local courthouse, passing a memorial that listed names of his comrades, and remembering all of them whether he wanted to or not.

Johnnie Wickersham fits perfectly into this changing world. By the time Wickersham wrote down his memories in 1915, he was a member of a dwindling class of Civil War veterans in the nation. The 1890 census, which included an attempt to canvass Civil War veterans in the nation, showed a total of 432,020 Confederate veterans still living. By 1900 that number had dwindled to 300,000. It was just 190,000 in 1910 and had fallen to approximately 75,000 by 1922.[5] Much the same as with World War II veterans today, it became a matter of intense interest to the larger society (those who had not made the sacrifice) for each individual veteran to tell his story before it was too late.

Johnnie Wickersham's tale is an excellent representation of the attitudes of the Old South, Lost Cause, and New South filtered through the lens of the passage of fifty years. He begins by focusing on the reconciliation of North and South as seen through his eyes during a trip to Canada. Throughout his work he speaks of the valor of soldiers, especially Confederates. The older Johnnie Wickersham has lived through not only the war itself but also fifty years of seeing his war experience changed into something mythical. It is no surprise that his memoir reflects those myths as well as the realities of war.

Wickersham's memoir reflects many of the stereotypes of Southern thought, especially in regard to race. He refers to African Americans as "darkies" and "negroes"; the slaves he encounters are all happy with their lives, love their masters, and are eager to help the young Rebel shine. I have left this language unchanged. Wickersham also recreates a great deal of dialogue, much of which he could not have heard firsthand. Again, I have left these recollections unchanged. Wickersham's voice is heard throughout as it should be, although punctuation has been corrected. Errors in spelling (where not confusing) or in the historical facts have been left in place, though the latter, where possible, are annotated to provide clarity as to the actual names, places, and events to which he refers. The sole organizational change was to create chapters within the manuscript to provide a more structured narrative flow.

Johnnie Wickersham went to war as a child. He returned home four years later, having seen much more death and destruction than most people do in a lifetime. As the decades passed, he transferred the war experience into a living example of memory and myth combined. And his memoir is an excellent reminder of how truth and fact can change over time, even for those who lived the events they describe.

Wickersham was just fourteen years old when he left his Lebanon, Missouri, home in 1861 and followed his two older brothers to war. For the next four years, he had the typical experiences of both a teenager and a Confederate soldier. He enjoyed his first kiss and killed his first man. He attacked Sherman's communication lines and served as a companion for a Union prisoner's younger sister. "Captain" Johnnie met generals and slaves. Wickersham's memoir, which he titled "The Gray and the Blue," is a combined war memoir and coming-of-age story.

Before the Civil War, the Wickersham family was probably remarkable only for its wealth. Johnnie Wickersham was born to Isaac and Nancy in Kentucky in 1846. The family already included Sarah, born in 1832; Richard, born in 1834; and James, born in 1840. By the time Johnnie was two years old, his entire family had traveled west, first to Illinois and then to Missouri. The group who made the move to Missouri from Illinois included his parents, siblings, and Richard's wife and child. In addition, the family took their two slaves, Wallace and Frank. They settled in Lebanon, Missouri, in

1857. Isaac bought 160 acres in the area and settled in to build both his business and his home. However, he did it without his wife, Nancy, who died in 1859. In his memoir, Wickersham writes that Isaac was a successful dry goods merchant, but this description seems to be an understatement. The 1870 census lists Isaac as owning real estate worth twenty-five thousand dollars and personal property worth another eight hundred dollars (illustrating both Isaac's personal success and the lack of damage the Civil War did to Lebanon). If he were not the richest man in the little town, he was close to it. He also bought and sold horses and had brought a large number of them from Kentucky. His sons' experience with horses served them well during the war. It is not surprising, given their backgrounds, that the Wickershams supported the Confederacy and the two oldest brothers went to war as soon as they could. Johnnie ran away in the middle of the night to join them, overcoming his father's initial opposition to having all his sons away at war.[6]

Johnnie spent most of the war with one or the other of his brothers. Richard and James served together in the Laclede (Lebanon) Company of the Third Infantry Regiment of the Seventh Division of the Missouri State Guards. Richard was the company commander, and James Craig (probably the Joe Crawford of the memoir), James H. Wickersham, and Charles Ketchum were the lieutenants. They spent most of 1861 and early 1862 in Missouri and Arkansas. The unit saw its first major action in March 1862 at the battle of Pea Ridge, where they were forced to retreat in that Confederate defeat. After the Missouri State Guard disbanded in early 1862, Richard and James Wickersham served in different units for the duration of the war. James was with the Fourth Missouri Infantry, which permanently became the First and Fourth Missouri Consolidated Infantry in November 1862.

He started with the unit as a first lieutenant in Company E and ended as a captain. Company E fought with General Daniel Frost's artillery brigade at Pea Ridge and then spent most of 1863 and 1864 in Mississippi, including the siege of Vicksburg. The unit was part of the Atlanta campaign, fought at Franklin, Tennessee, and surrendered May 4, 1865.[7]

Tracing Richard Wickersham is harder. When the war ended he was a lieutenant colonel in Colonel Robert Wood's Regiment. This group was formed by July 1863 and was in Arkansas by July 27. Wood's Regiment was technically unattached, although it was assigned to Brigadier General John S. Marmaduke's cavalry division. The unit spent much of the war in Arkansas and participated in General Sterling Price's 1864 raid into Missouri. Wood's Regiment surrendered at Shreveport, Louisiana, in May 1865.[8]

Besides serving with his brothers, Johnnie occasionally also had other duties. He was as an orderly for General Price and accompanied Richard on a raid back into Missouri. His unit missed the battle of Shiloh, arriving there shortly after it was over. For a good portion of 1862 Wickersham was at a place he calls "Fairyland" with Colonel Colton Greene. This was a plantation apparently owned by a Mexican War veteran and friend of Greene's. Greene used this time as a recovery period from the war. Although it is difficult to determine the exact location of this plantation, it most likely was in northern Mississippi. Greene eventually sent Wickersham to carry messages to General Kirby Smith, and Wickersham rejoined his unit during the siege of Vicksburg. Shortly after Greene sent Wickersham on his way, the plantation and its owners were captured by the Union. Along with most of his comrades, Wickersham was captured at Vicksburg and sent to a parole camp (where captured units were held until allowed back to duty) at Demopolis, Alabama. After the unit was paroled, Wickersham went to Dalton, Georgia, and joined General John Bell Hood in battling Sherman in and outside Atlanta. He also helped watch over the sister of a wounded Union soldier until he was ordered back to duty. Wickersham participated in raids against Sherman's railroad and supply lines after Atlanta fell. As a reward for his role in "hazardous duty," he was allowed to take the unit's mail back to Missouri.

It is during his trip back home (in late 1864) that the reader is reminded once again that he was not much more than a child even after three bloody years. Wickersham is thrilled to go to a circus in the company of young girls, meets a childhood rival, and runs away. The trip home to Missouri and then back to his unit is a long, harrowing one, and he finally rejoins his group in Mississippi. Wickersham fights the few remaining months with his unit and surrenders with them in New Orleans in May 1865. Once again he has to make the long trip back home and seemingly magically finds his family. The abrupt ending of his story leaves many questions unanswered.

After the war, Wickersham resumed his life in Missouri. He married Nancy Stoddard in April 1874 in Jasper, Missouri, and they had a son, Austin, in October 1875. A year and a half later on February 21, 1877, their daughter, Helen, was born. A second son, John, was born three years after Helen. The family lived in Clinton, Missouri, as late as 1895. Helen married Curtis Wright in Carthage, Missouri, in 1903 and was the mother of the Curtis for whom this memoir was written. Sometime before 1910, Curtis took a job at the Pacific Bed Spring Company in Berkeley, California. Johnnie, his wife, and Austin all went west with Curtis and his family.[9] The 1910 census shows Wickersham's profession as traveling salesman and that he was living in Berkeley with his wife.

Wickersham died there in November 1916. He was survived by his wife and children. Nancy lived until 1931, and Austin until 1952.

Wickersham wrote this memoir in 1915, shortly before his death. It was apparently at the urging of his family that he recorded his memories. Wickersham had been entertaining his relatives with war stories for years, and they wanted to have them all written down before he was gone. Copies were privately printed for family members, and a few remain in libraries. A portion was also published by the Arkansas Historical Society's journal, *The Stream of History,* in January 1969. Sections may also be found in a work by noted folklorist B. A. Botkin, *A Civil War Treasury of Tales, Legends and Folklore.* The memoir came to my attention through a descendant of Curtis Wright, Rebecca Pierce, my colleague at Minnesota State University, Mankato.

The passage of fifty years between the end of the Civil War and Wickersham putting his memories on paper accounts for some rather serious problems. Wickersham makes mistakes about names and dates. He recounts conversations that could not have occurred when and where he says they did. It has proven impossible to confirm some of the events he describes. The most troubling of these is Wickersham's description of his role in attacking Sherman's lines outside Atlanta. Only a few pieces of evidence confirm any part of it. James Wickersham was assigned to a special unit commanded by Colonel Hill (as Johnnie claims) at this time. *The Official Records* mention a special unit (led by Hill) assigned to harass Sherman's transportation and communication lines. But without more substantive evidence it is impossible to say anything stronger than that it is likely something similar to what Wickersham describes happened. This episode is emblematic of the promise and problems of this memoir.

There are enough questions that one has to wonder whether some aspects of the work are a fairy tale. But because there are sufficient ways to substantiate most of it, it seems far more likely that Wickersham's memory was tricking him after so long. This memoir reflects not only the war years but also the many changes Confederate veterans experienced in the decades after Appomattox. Fifty years after the war, many veterans from both sides were facing old age and death. They worried that their stories would not be told or would be usurped by those who had not actually been there. But the tales they related were influenced by what happened in the fifty years after the war.

By the time Wickersham actually wrote his memories down, the fiftieth anniversary of the war's biggest battles had come and gone. Even living on the West Coast, Wickersham would have heard of President Woodrow Wilson's trip to the Gettysburg Battlefield to preside over the reunion of Confederate and Union veterans and his speech emphasizing that the former enemies were now allies. The more than fifty-three thousand veterans who attended the reunion were both living symbols of the nation's most tragic and heroic moment and a sign that the United States was united once again. Wickersham, the former boy hero, was one of them, even three thousand miles away, and his memoir clearly reflects the heroic version of the war that had been widely accepted by both scholars and the general public in the five decades since Appomattox.[10]

Wickersham starts his story by telling of the years after the war, a sign that he was aware that those years were as important in his storytelling as the war years. He begins with a discussion of the reconciliation of North and South, the maturing of the nation, and the maturing of the child who was Johnnie Wickersham, boy soldier. This beginning fits in perfectly with what David Blight calls the "Reconciliation" phase of Civil War memory that began in the 1890s. Early on in Wickersham's story, just as in the nation as a whole, the uniting of North and South took center stage and the debate over the causes of the war itself disappeared (especially any discussion of racial tension). The memoir is a picaresque tale, an old man remembering the boy he once was; the boy forever lost to four years of bloody warfare and fifty years of seeing those four years transformed into something magical and mythical.

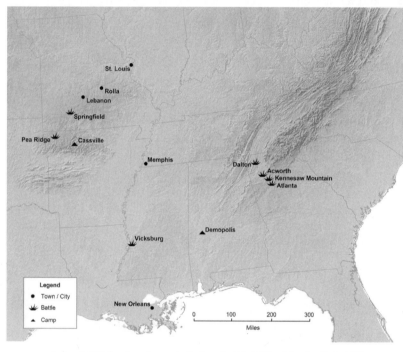

Johnnie Wickersham's travels during the Civil War. Map by C. A. Miller, Department of Geography, Minnesota State University, Mankato.

Boy Soldier of the Confederacy

Prologue
The Gray and the Blue

At the solicitation of both family and comrades, but more particularly for the benefit of my ten-year-old Grandson, Curtis Wright III, I have tried to inscribe in the following pages for him and those who may come after him such personal incidents as memory permits me to retain of my boyhood life in the Army of the South during our Civil War.

I was less than fifteen years old when I ran away from home and joined the Army. The tragic events of that period have indelibly printed on memory's tablet pictures that only death can efface, the mind recalls them more clearly than it does incidents of recent date.

I have not attempted a description of great battles or the strategic movement of armies but only the true personal escapades of a boy that are known, told, retold, and discussed by all the members of the family around the fireside of your Grandfather.

1

"Memory Seems So Real"

You, my little Grandson, are the descendant of both North and South and have in you the making of the highest type of a true American citizen. Your Grandfather on your Father's side fought for the Blue, and your Grandfather on your Mother's side fought for the Gray. I was too young to judge of the justice of either cause, but looking backward after more than fifty years, I feel that under our system of government then, with the doctrine of States Rights paramount to that of the National Government, any man living south of Mason and Dixon's Line who did not defend his state from invasion was as much a traitor to his state as one who living north did not take up arms for his government.

Now that the War is but a memory, time has healed all our wounds. We Grandfathers know no North or South, East or West but vie with each other in our endeavors to show our allegiance to our united glorious country. I hope, Curtis, this same spirit will animate you and your descendants. In being true to your father and his people and your mother and her people, you have a grave responsibility forced upon you, and more, much more, will be expected of you. You must always maintain the honor and pride of both North and South, never permitting yourself to become the partisan of one against the other.

I will relate a little incident that will perhaps illustrate my feelings:

Some time ago I made a trip through Canada. The customs and habits of the Canadians are different from ours. It would be impolite to speak to one without passing through the formality of an introduction; so if I wanted to talk, had to do most of it to myself.

Finally I reached Vancouver, B.C. It happened to be Fete Week, and from every telephone and telegraph pole floated the Canadian Flag or the Union Jack; buildings covered with unfamiliar bunting, soldiers marching, and bands playing "God Save the King" made me feel like a man without a country, until I spied through the flags and bunting four blocks away "Old Glory" waving from a window. Unconsciously my hat came off, bareheaded I walked, and up the stairs a young man met me at the railing of our Consul's office. "I wish to see the American Consul," I said. A white-haired officer who had lost a leg in the Civil War heard me and, taking his crutch, came to the railing saying, "I am the American Consul. What can I do for you?" I said, "Comrade, give me your hand. I fought four years against that old flag hanging out the window yonder, but you don't love or reverence it a bit more than I do." He swung open the gate, and I found a friend, as I always have from the true soldier that wore the Blue.

We all now realize that we were a very foolish nation in 1861. We were not fighting enemies, but brothers, reared under the same influence, with the same hopes and aspirations, often of the same blood. Even our own family was divided, and we fought to kill each other. Your life is full of your schoolmate and you last week were good friends, one accuses the other of wrongdoing, you have a fight—this week, arm in arm you go to school and your respect for each other is even greater than before.

The following are memory's vivid pictures of youth that the "Good Master" permits us older people to retain. The incidents here described occurred more than a half century ago. The life pictures of my youth are so indelibly photographed on my brain at that time, have lain sealed and forgotten all these years, yet as I write, the mind compels memory to unlock her storehouse. They are not the cold, colorless pictures of the photographer but the real living pictures of my youth. Memory seems so real, the pictures so vivid, that I am again a boy in Gray and the tears come as I linger amid scenes of the bloody conflict.

FAMILY SKETCH

As you know, we were Kentucky people for many generations. When I was two years old, my father took his family to live in St. Louis, where he accumulated what was considered quite a fortune in those days. His business was buying horses and mules and shipping them South, and even from a little tot I was at home on almost any horse's back. I was awarded first prize for the best boy rider at the St. Louis County Fair. Father, in 1857, sold all his St. Louis properties and bought large tracts of land in what was then a most thinly settled section of the country in and near the Village of Lebanon in Southwest Missouri. There was a farm with town house given to each of my two brothers and two sisters. The home place was intended to be mine.

There was much excitement during the preparations for our moving. In those days such a move was considered a great undertaking. Father had seventy head of horses, largely brood mares. I remember, particularly, Nickbiddle, Blackhawk, and his imported Belgian horse Norman, also a drove of blooded cattle. In that great caravan were five buffaloes, besides household furniture and merchandise for a general store. My two brothers started weeks ahead and drove the stock over land more than two hundred miles to Rolla, the terminus of the railroad. The women, father, and I went by rail to Rolla; and thence one hundred miles over the roughest mountain road you could imagine to Lebanon, Missouri. To a city bred child, the country seemed a paradise. With joy and gladness in my heart, every morning on my horse with gun across the pommel of my saddle, I was sent to the prairies herding stock. At nightfall I usually untied a string of prairie chickens or quail from my saddle. Undoubtedly this life in the open air went far toward making me physically able to withstand the hardships and privations I underwent during the war.

WHY I BECAME A REBEL

Lebanon, Missouri, was the most secluded, isolated little community you could imagine, one hundred miles from railroad or telegraph. Newspapers were rare and so old when they reached us that we knew but little of the contention and agitation that was exciting the rest of the country. We heard only sufficient to make gossip for the loungers on the dry goods box at the country store. We heard talk of war but never dreamed it would reach us or that there were soldiers on either side near us. So you cannot in any manner conceive of the surprise, alarm, and excitement caused by seeing the old lane, a mile and a half away on the Rolla road, filled with soldiers, their bayonets gleaming in the sunlight. "Who are they?," "What are they doing here?" was on everyone's tongue. On they came, and as they marched into town, we learned they were General Lyon's advance guard of three regiments of German United States troops, in command of General Seigel, on their way to fight General Price at Wilson Creek, near Springfield, Missouri.[1] Few of them could speak English. They immediately arrested and put in jail all able-bodied men, my brother Dick among the number. Brother Jim hid out in the brush, and I carried provisions to him. I was so small they did not molest me, and I went among them, learning what I could to tell the frightened women and men in hiding. I saw them drive big army wagons to my father's store, and when they drove away there were only empty shelves left. They took every head of stock my father owned, except three most valuable horses, Norman, Nickbiddle, Blackhawk, and two saddle horses. They were in the barn, and when I discovered what was being done, I led them out to the woods and hid them in the small timber. Father sent me to a corn field more than two miles from town where he had eighty fat hogs and many sows and little pigs. I found them all dead, riddled with bullets by the German cavalry.

All citizens, whether in sympathy with the South or not, who did not voluntarily ask to take the oath of allegiance were proclaimed Rebels. The soldiers under General Seigel had permission to take or destroy their property. They took every advantage of this permission. If a man asked for a receipt or a paper showing his loss, he was put in jail. This was the cause of my joining the South. Brother Dick stayed in jail six weeks, when with friendly assistance he cut his way out and escaped to the woods.

After General Lyon's army reached Lebanon and General Seigel had moved on toward Springfield, we were treated much more kindly. The town was filled with soldiers coming and going. With much interest I watched them drill, particularly the Field Artillery at target practice. How they did brag and tell what they would do to the "Rebs" when they caught them. I seemed transformed into another boy. I had been the frail, petted baby of the family and almost girlish in my disposition, but words came to my lips, "I'll fight them," "I'll fight them," and when I reached home father said, "Johnnie, what are you crying about?" I could only say, "I'll fight them," "I'll fight them," and for many days the words passed my lips unconsciously. The time came when the entire army had passed on towards Springfield, and then how quiet and peaceful it seemed. The town looked as if some great hurricane had passed through it.

FIRING AT WILSON CREEK

About three weeks later, on a bright Sunday that I shall never forget, it seemed that everybody was at the Methodist Church. What the preacher was saying I do not remember, but I remember that in the midst of the service someone tiptoed in and whispered to my father. Father followed him out of the church and so did others, both men and women. Everyone knew that something most unusual had occurred, as none came back. Finally I took courage and slipped out. My boy, you cannot imagine my fear and consternation when I saw my father and every man and woman lying flat on the ground. Not a word was spoken, and I noticed they all had their ears to the ground. Frightened but curious, I also lay down. I could see or hear nothing, then I felt the earth tremble, and I knew it was the ground vibration of the artillery firing at Wilson Creek, nearly fifty miles away. This was on the tenth of August! I remember the date from the old War Song that later became one of our camp songs: "T'was on the tenth of August we made the Lyon roar / The musket and the minnie balls around our tents did pour," etc. etc.[2]

We all went back into the church. Such serious looking people. I wanted to shout but dared not. The preacher said,

"Brother Wickersham will you lead us in prayer?" I wish I could remember that prayer. I knew how I stood but had never heard my father express himself. I knelt by his side looking up into his face, hoping, and when he prayed God to give victory to the South, I stood up and cried "Amen" so loudly it was moments before he could continue his prayer.

THE DEFEAT AND DEATH OF GENERAL LYON

Many of the men and women sat up and talked the night through—wondering who had won. Three days passed. They seemed like weeks. Finally a man came galloping into town, shouting the news that General Lyon was killed and the Yankees were defeated—most of them captured with their cannon and wagons—what was left of them would be in Lebanon in a few hours—General Price was just behind, and a battle was expected every minute.[3]

The town was wild with suppressed joy and fear. I remember everybody spake in whispers. Then came the Seigel men that we knew so well, in advance, but not with the pomp and arrogance of a few weeks before. They were raw troops, and my dear boy, may you never know what defeat and retreat means to untried, green soldiers. They had virtually run fifty miles—thrown away coats, haversacks and many had no guns. The look in their eyes I will never forget. Their clothes were wet with perspiration and covered with dust. When the command "halt" was given, every man fell to the ground. Price was not following, but they thought he was, and it had the same effect. They could rest but one hour. The bugle sounded, and with tired, weary legs and sore feet, they started on that long tramp of one hundred miles to Rolla. Their wagons carried only the wounded—their horses were exhausted. They did no foraging, had no stragglers, and by ten o'clock the next day the entire army had passed on.

When we had ascertained that there were no more to come, we uncorked our suppressed joy and made the Welkin ring with praises to God.

A COMPANY FOR THE SOUTH

Brother Dick came back—Jim came to town, and from all over the country came men with their squirrel rifles and shotguns. They organized on the Public Square a large company for the South, electing Brother Dick Captain; Joe Crawford, First Lieutenant; and Brother Jim, Second Lieutenant.[4] They were mostly young men who had spent their lives in the open—physically strong and crack shots. Had it not been for the conduct of General Seigel and his men, probably not more than one in ten of these would have cast his lot with the South.

Accustomed to the equipment and discipline of our regular army of today, you cannot imagine what an unsoldierly appearance this company made, with their peaceful hunting guns, powder horns, and bullet molds. The contrast with the soldiers of General Lyon's army stood in bold relief. There were no feathers in their hats, no brass buttons, no bands of music, or loud command; but when they left for the South the Captain simply said, "Come on, boys." Their clothes were homemade and of every color. They had no flag. The ladies wished to make them one but could find no person who knew what the Rebel flag was.

In the morning, with three wagons loaded with crude cooking utensils, provisions, but no tents, they started to find General Price's army. They heard he was at Springfield, Missouri.

I RUN AWAY FROM HOME

How I begged to go. My brothers were angry that I should think of such a thing. Dick said, "If you mention that again,

I will take you across my knee." Then I went to my father. He sympathized with me and understood me much better than my brothers but said it was out of reason—that I was not yet fifteen and they would drive me out of camp. We talked far into the night, and when I was in bed he knelt and prayed and kissed me. But my mind was made up. When he left and the house was quiet, I stole quietly downstairs, took the old rifle from the deer-horns in the hall, saddled my horse in the barn, and started south. By making inquiries and watching the trail, I had no difficulty in finding my way. In a few hours I would reach them.

MY OLD FATHER

I looked back and in a cloud of dust saw a horseman coming at full speed. It proved to be my father. That was the first great crisis of my life. To his entreaties I had only one answer, "If you make me go back, Father, I will run away again." Without a word but with tears in his eyes, he unstrapped a package on the back of his saddle and when he had unwrapped it, he handed me the most beautiful little gun I had ever seen. It was in two pieces, and he showed me how to put it together. It was breech-loading and proved to be a Maynard rifle.[5] How I thanked and kissed him for it! He took my big gun, and we got down on our knees in that dusty road, and he prayed as I had never heard him pray before. He took me in his arms. Then he mounted and rode away, leaving me alone in the road. Alone but Oh! so happy! Half an hour before I had been a runaway boy, but now I was a man going with my father's blessing to defend my State, and in my arms I held the rifle he had given me.

I came upon the Command some twenty miles from Springfield, much to the disgust and annoyance of my brothers, but the other boys gave me a hearty welcome. Other companies of the "Web-foot" (Infantry) found us, and when we reached Springfield we numbered some two hundred and forty men. All along our march there came men on horseback in squads of from four to ten. They were unorganized, and I remember that few had guns.[6]

SPRINGFIELD

When we reached Springfield, to our great surprise, we found that General Price and his army had hurriedly retreated some time before. We went into camp in an old pasture a mile south of town.

We stood our guns against the fence and hung our powder horns to the stakes.

We were ignorant of war: it being more like a gathering of country folk bent on having a frolic. Bordering the pasture on the south was a dense growth of scrub oaks, whose trunks were about the size of my arm. In front (east) was the county road with its ten-rail staked and double-ridered fence forming a continuous lane from Springfield to the Fair Grounds, a mile and a half to the south. Towards Springfield the pasture sloped downward to a small creek some six hundred yards away.

A wide gap was made in the rail fences in our front, so we could cross the lane to a spring in the pasture beyond.

HORSE RACING

We had barely settled into camp before the boys were trying the running qualities of their horses. Horse racing in those days was our most fascinating sport, and the lane was like the race-track at our county fairs. As the horses raced, we boys afoot lined the top rider of the fence like blackbirds and yelled and cheered them as they passed by.

CAPTURE OF MAJOR WHITE

About three o'clock in the afternoon, our officers, with the exception of Lieutenant Joe Crawford, rode into Springfield; I followed afoot, and a great surprise awaited us. We found that some of our men on horseback (you could not call them cavalry in those days) had captured a Yankee major named White of General Fremont's body guard.[7] He was a sight to our uneducated eyes, literally covered with gold braid from head to foot; the wonder he created among us can only be imagined. All we could learn was he had taken the wrong road and was lost. I might here tell you something of General Fremont's body-guard taken from official report.

FREMONT'S BODY-GUARD

To become a member of this select organization of four hundred and eighty men, one had to be six feet or over, pass strict physical examination, and have a full military mustache. Their clothing was made from the finest cloth covered with ornaments and gold braid. Their large hats were black felt with a great gold cord and tassel with black ostrich plume. Besides his sword, each had swung from his shoulder a four-inch fair-leather belt attached to which was a silver plated gun-stock or breech. Each had a pair of holsters fastened to the horn of his saddle containing a Colt Army Dragoon six-chamber, silver-plated made to attach to the stock or breech.[8]

The command had stopped at a distillery, five miles from Springfield, and after filling their stomachs with peach brandy, had filled the canteen that was contained in his unique stock or breech. Many could scarcely keep their saddles. The trappings with saddles and bridles equaled those of a circus parade. General Fremont was reprimanded for spending so much money on this body-guard. They surpassed in pomp and grandeur anything ever seen in an army.

I FORGOT MY ORDERS

We never dreamed that the enemy was near us. Dick spied me down in town and told me to go back to camp and tell the boys to get their guns; that they had captured a Yankee major and there might be troops about. When I reached the mouth of the lane, I waited for the finish of a horse race before going on. Upon reaching the camp we heard the clatter of horses's feet beyond the usual starting point of our races.

BIG RACE

A man of the fence shouted, "Big race, seven horses in it." Instantly the men left me and climbed the fence. I forgot my orders and in a moment was on the top rider and, like all the rest, was waving my hat and shouting encouragement at the top of my voice to the riders, particularly to a man on a gray horse who was a little behind. "I'll bet two bits on the bay," shouted my neighbor. (That was the limit of betting in those days.) Every man was on the fence excepting a very few who were not interested in racing. Before the dust of the seven horses, that we later learned were those of our frightened pickets, had cleared away, came eighty men, the Yankee advance guard, eight abreast with sabers drawn and plumes flying.

"Law, what pretty men," the boys yelled. Every one of us was now on the top rider of the fence, cheering and yelling in our mad excitement at the gold and silver men passing on horses. Many stood up on the fence and waved and yelled as long as they were in sight. Not a soul thought of war or fighting.

THE FIGHT

Before they had passed from view, the main body of four hundred had wheeled in our front and commenced firing at us. "You gol-darned fools," the boys shouted, "cut that out, you'll hit some of us with your blamed foolishness." Others said, "Say, are you fellows from Price's army?" Lieutenant Crawford jumped on the fence, waving his sword, and shouted, "Boys, get your guns, they are Yankees." Fortunately for us they were over drilled. They fired by command and in platoons, raising those big revolvers over their shoulders, at the same time cocking them, and at the word "Fire," pulled the triggers and over shot us.

In this first part of the fight, the only men that were hit were the ones without curiosity or interest in the horse race. No words of mine, my boy, can give you any idea how Lieutenant Crawford's words electrified us. Instantly every man dropped from the fence and found a gun. Through the opening between the rails the clear crack of the squirrel rifle, or the deeper detonation of the shot gun, filled every man with the ecstacy of excitement and joy. Four hundred of the enemy crowded between the two fences, almost against the muzzles of our guns, the front line using their sabers, cutting at our men over the fence.

There was no fear; it all came upon us like a flash of lightning. We plain country folks were then like wild animals at the first taste of blood. "I got the big fellow, look at him falling," cried a neighbor boy. "My God," said another, "look at the dead horses." The enemy were a brave lot and stayed until each had fired twelve shots at us. They passed on to the creek towards town, where they formed a junction with their advance guard. The lane seemed filled with dead and wounded men and horses. Then came the scramble for every man to find his own gun and get his powder and balls ready, for we believed they would come back, and they did.

Again from towards town, eight abreast, they wheeled into line against the fence, riding over the dead and wounded, and the same battle was repeated, but much more fatally to both sides. A man by the name of McCall, by my side, after he had fired his gun, could not find his powder flask. In his frenzy he climbed on top of the fence and with the butt of his gun unhorsed one of the enemy. The poor fellow was cut to pieces by the sabers.[9] My attention was attracted to some sixty of the enemy that were outside the lane, in perfect line, about sixty yards away, using their dragoon revolvers as guns. They fired at will and did good execution.

How plain that picture is to me today. It does not seem possible, and yet I shouted with joy as I saw them fall from their saddles. About twenty of our riflemen with a rest on the fence made many a shot tell. They left many men and horses on that knoll. The fighting lasted until each had fired twelve shots, and then they ran toward the Fair Grounds. Ten, fifteen, twenty minutes passed, and we thought they were gone. We found we had many killed and wounded and were caring for them. A straggler came running, saying they were forming for another charge at the Fair Grounds.

I might say here that in the scramble and excitement, I could not find my little "Maynard Rifle" but grabbed the first gun I found leaning against the fence. Fortunately it had powder horn and bullets tied to it. It was all right when I had the fence to rest it on, but I could not hold it off-hand.

Lieutenant Crawford foolishly formed the line thirty yards back from the fence. He made us a speech; positive orders for no one to fire without his command. I was the smallest, and, as was usual in those days, my place was at the tail end of the line, or nearest Springfield, and immediately in front of where the fence was down. From my position, I could see as far as the Fair Grounds and I saw them in the road forming. They started in a walk.

I was wild with the ecstasy of it all, for I was too young to appreciate the danger. I danced and shouted, "They are coming, coming." The men said, "Shut up, you little fool," etc., etc., but I heard them not. They were coming now in a trot, a big officer on a magnificent prancing horse leading them, his sword flashing in the sunlight. He shouted his orders, but I could not understand him. As they came nearer I heard, "Charge the gap, charge the gap." Thirty yards in my immediate front was the gap. I turned and shouted down the line, "They are going to charge the gap." I never knew what made me, but I ran to within ten paces of the gap, knelt down with elbow on my knee and rifle at my shoulder, waiting. The men swore and cursed me, but I did not heed them. I was unconscious of what I was doing.

On they came; not a shot was fired. The officer wheeled into the gap. The advance had passed through, and as the officer raised his sword to strike me, my rifle rang out; the bullet pierced his breast. I had never used a profane word before in my life, but the men said I threw down my gun and danced and swore like a trooper. I was oblivious to my surroundings. I did not hear the hundreds shout, "Lie down, you little fool." Lieutenant Crawford gave the command "Fire," but I did not hear it. My man was down, his horse had stopped. One foot was still in the stirrup. I worked it loose and tied the horse, then I went back to him and made him as comfortable as possible. He tried to say something to me, but I could not understand him. He was a very large man, and I had much difficulty unbuckling his sword belt and getting it off. His sword was still fastened to his wrist by a braided leather cord, and it took me several minutes to get it loose. I tried to hold the sword out, and when I stood it up by me it was nearly as tall as I. I remember he wore a fine diamond and much jewelry. No power on earth could have induced me to even touch these things, but his sword, pistols and horse were mine by the rules of war and I would have fought the world for them.[10]

MY TROPHIES

I left him and went to the horse. He was a beauty. His saddle and bridle were the most magnificent I had ever seen. There were funny looking things on the horn of the saddle, and I found they contained two silver plated dragoon revolvers. Both were loaded. I had never seen such pistols.[11] I was so fascinated with my trophies I forgot the fighting going on all around me. I came to myself when I heard the shout of our boys and learned afterwards that we had defeated them for the third time in the lane; that the gap was almost blocked with dead horses and men; and that they had gone to the creek towards town and let down the fence and made the great "Charge of Zegonia" in history, and driven our boys back to the scrub oaks previously mentioned. Horsemen, no matter how brave and gallant, cannot compete with squirrel rifles and shot guns in thick timber. I was unconscious of the charge that swept by me, sabring some of our men before they could reach the brush, and only came back to earth when I heard the Rebel yell of victory. I looked up and saw the Yankees running in every direction to get out of range of the deadly fire of our men. I was standing in front of the gap with one of those most wonderful pistols in each hand. I saw our boys come out of the brush, firing at the running Federals. To my surprise a body of about thirty was trying to escape by way of the gap. In my boyish ignorance I yelled to them to come on. They came. My fire checked the leaders, the ones behind ran over them. It was a miracle the horses did not trample me to death. When the boys found me I was lying unconscious from a blow on the head, but tightly grasped in each hand was my first spoils of war, the two silver mounted Dragoon revolvers with only one chamber not fired. One of them now lies on my desk as I write. More than a half century of time has changed its silver plating to dull brass, but not so with memory. If I shut my eyes on the present as I close my fingers around the butt of the old gun, I feel again the same thrill that shook the little fifteen year old Johnnie Reb when he foolishly tried to hold the gap alone against Zegonia's Charge. To you, my little grandson, I give my most cherished relic of the war.

THE JUST PUNISHMENT OF A COWARD

There was a very unpopular man in our Command. He was always telling what he would do when he got a chance at the "Yanks." He was not only a braggart but a coward. During the entire fight he hid in the brush, but when he found the enemy was gone, he came out of hiding. Approaching a group of prisoners, he deliberately shot and killed one. Lieutenant Crawford, who was standing by, without a word drew his sword and with one stroke almost severed his head from his body. After the war was over Lieutenant Crawford was sent to prison for this act and did not get out until years after, when he was pardoned by the governor.[12]

LEAVING FOR PRICE'S ARMY

We left most of our frying pans, skillets, and plunder, and loaded our wagons with the wounded, and started again to find General Price, who was in Arkansas. The men pulled the dead men and horses out of the gap and lane, and piled them together against the fence on either side so our wagons could pass, and about ten o'clock that dark night, we started. Several of our officers had come back. I noticed my brother Jim among them. He, with others, had taken refuge in the

Court House in town, and had made a gallant fight. Jim took charge of some thirty men as a rear guard. The night was very dark. The men on horseback at the beginning of the fight had "struck for the tall timber," but now they were coming back in bunches. They disturbed us greatly as we could not tell in the dark whether they were enemies or friends. The foolish boys who had guns kept firing.

THE STAMPEDE

The road ran through a very large prairie. To the right and parallel with the road was a ravine with almost perpendicular banks about ten feet high. We had some twenty or thirty horsemen behind the rear guard. Suddenly, out of the darkness came a large body of horsemen yelling and firing as they came.

The horsemen in our rear, thinking they were the enemy, stampeded and broke through the rear guard, before Brother Jim had ordered his men to fire in order to save ourselves from being trampled. Several were killed. The larger body on their mad, plunging horses, rode over us, men and wagons, and most of us were forced into the ravine. All were more or less stunned by the fall. In the confusion many prisoners escaped.

When I recovered consciousness I found near me two horses with the wagon on top of them. I was among some thirty prisoners, and in my dazed condition I was sure the Yankee cavalry had come back and defeated our men. I started to crawl out to escape when I saw a man with a lantern in the ditch ordering the prisoners out. I believed him to be a Yankee officer. Then others came out and they began taking the men up. The man with the lantern approached me. I was lying on my face holding my breath, he felt my pulse and threw my hand down on the hard ground but I did not flinch. He said, "This poor boy is dead." Several men were mixed up under the horses and wagons, and as he held my lantern high I saw his face. Joy came to my heart, and I shouted, "Hello, Dr. Britts." Dr. Britts was a dear friend, and not only during the war but for many years after, we laughed over this incident.[13]

Long before we reached General Price's army the news of our fight was the talk of the camp. Men love to magnify the deeds of a boy. Everybody was my friend, and all exaggerated what I had done.

2

"The First Time I Heard 'Dixie'"

COMMISSIONED CAPTAIN

The second day after we had reached the army an orderly came with the command for me to report to General Price's headquarters. You can imagine how surprised I was. I found a fatherly, white-haired old man, with such a kindly look, so entirely different from what I had imagined the great soldier to be that I was not afraid and walked right up to him. He took my hand, and I stood by him all the time I was there. He asked me many questions. I did not feel that I had done anything unusual. I told him about the fight, and he laughed most heartily.

He turned to Colonel Sneed, his Adjutant General, and said, "Write out a commission to Captain Johnnie Wickersham."[1] I could not grasp the full meaning of it. I was ordered to report every day at headquarters. When I went back to the boys they all wanted to know why General Price had sent for me. I said, "He gave me this paper with this big seal on it." The men danced and shouted and embarrassed me by waiting on me with exaggerated respect and said that a captain must not do anything for himself. Whatever I wanted done I must tell them. It took me a long time to become accustomed to my new honors.

MY UNIFORM

Colonel Colton Green took charge of me.[2] One day I was ordered to his tent. He told me to strip and put on the clothes I found there. Where he got it I never knew, but it was a Confederate Captain's uniform and fitted me perfectly. I was proud, and yet I did not feel I deserved the honor they were giving me, but I tried to wear it with the dignity that I knew they expected. Everybody who heard of me magnified what I had done, and every soldier saluted me. How I wished they would not! I had my blooded bay horse with all his trappings. Thinking of it today, I must have been a caricature; a little slender boy in an officer's gorgeous uniform on that big horse with that big saddle.

The regiment was on parade, the fife and drum corps was playing.[3] Colonel Green ordered me to ride with him to the front. The regiment was at "present arms," and Colonel Green made the men a speech. Turning, he presented me with a beautiful pearl handled sword. It was small but of exquisite workmanship. It was lost in the surrender of Vicksburg.

The army stayed at Cassville, Arkansas, some time, drilling, burning charcoal to make powder, and molding bullets. The routine of camp life grew monotonous to me. I was Captain but had no command, no duties to perform, and could go and come at will. I remember Colonel Colton Green sent a man to the guard house for swearing in my presence. He and Colonel Emmett McDonald were as careful of me as if I were a girl.[4]

MY FIRST EXPERIENCE AS A SCOUT

Brother Dick was Captain of General Price's Scouts. General Price ordered him to go alone as far as he could toward Rolla in order to find out if any troops were in or beyond Lebanon. I was homesick and begged that I might go with him. I appealed to General Price, and then Dick surprised me by saying he would like to have me. Oh! Curtis, you can not imagine how happy—yes, and proud, too, I was to be on my horse, with my fine pistols, out in the woods and prairies again. Brother Dick treated me so differently, almost as an equal. Of this I think I was more proud than of anything that had happened. It seemed to me that we rode everywhere. How far or how long I do not remember, but they were happy days. Dick, with all his daring, was cautious, and many times I held his horse while he crawled up to a house for information.

Finally we reached the Lebanon section of the country. How uneasy and restless I grew as I held the horses and waited the night through for Dick to return. Just at daylight he came back. He had been into Lebanon. In answer to my questions he said, "No Johnnie, I'll not say a word until we both have something to eat. Then we will hold a council of war."

LANCERS

We ate our cold grub, and he laughingly told me there was only one company of Lancers in town but a large body of troops some miles beyond.[5] Some very foolish officers armed many Yankee companies at the beginning of the war with long hickory poles with a sharp steel spear on the end. We had seen an article in an old St. Louis Republican in which the writer claimed that in the first fight each Lancer would have a Reb at the end of his lance. Dick said they had six pickets out where I used to herd stock, and that we would have some fun tonight.

We tethered our horses and slept until past midnight.

Again we looked after our horses, ate our lunch, and started off. It was a dark night. Finally we dismounted and led our horses. Bill showed me the picket's camp fire, which had almost gone out, but it was a long way off.[6] We went down the hill and made a long detour, coming back to a hollow.

THE CHARGE

At last Bill whispered, "The pickets are three hundred yards to our right; look to your saddle girt; see that everything is right; follow me and do just what I do"—"Are you ready?" With spurs in the flanks of our surprised horses, we were off like a shot from a pistol. When we reached the knoll we gave the Rebel Yell and commenced firing. They thought the entire Rebel army was on them. The company in town heard the firing and fled. Bill sent me down one street while he went up another. We kept yelling, and in twenty minutes there was not a Lancer to be seen. It was dark, but we knew every part of the old town. Dick said he was going home. I rode my horse to Father's barn and gave him a big feed.

MY FIRST KISS

Then I went to Brother Dick's house. Mary, his wife, was in his arm, where she had jumped from bed at his call.[7] She gave me a great hug and said, "Little Lizzie Harrison is here." Although I had hoped for this, I had only enough courage to say "Howdy," but Lizzie said, "Oh! Captain Johnnie, won't you kiss me too?" I shall always remember this, my first kiss. How proud and vain I was to have Lizzie see me in my new gaudy uniform with feathers and gold braid.[8]

It was about daylight, so Mary gave us a fine breakfast and I started out to see my sister Sarah.[9] She was wild with joy to see me but scared almost to death, as she was nervous and excitable. "Johnnie, do please take off those big pistols,—they might go off and hurt you," she cried. Here it was that the boy in me made me strut and brag, and when I was in the midst of a boyish recital of my deeds of valor, little Lizzie Harrison came running with tears streaming down her cheeks crying, "Johnnie, Captain Johnnie, the lane is filled with bayonets, and the cavalry has surrounded the town." All the hilarity vanished. My horse was half a mile away in Father's stable. Sister Sarah and little Lizzie Harrison were on their knees begging me to surrender. The boy in me made me fold my arms and give them all a look of disgust as I slowly walked, or shall I say strutted, out of the house. But when I turned the corner I ran like the dickens for my horse.

MY FIRST GREAT SORROW

I put on the bridle and saddle and to my great horror discovered my horse was foundered, and I could not make him take even a single step. Dick was on his horse in the Public Square, firing to give me warning. How I wished my voice could reach him so that he could come and take me with him on his horse. I closed the stable door and fired one shot. He knew the loud report of my pistol, but instead of coming, two reports rang out from his pistol to let me know that he felt I was safe, and then he galloped away, never dreaming that I was not on my good horse and about to join him.

There are times, my boy, in the crisis even of a boy's life, when events and circumstances, temporarily at least, drive youth and laughter from his life. Again, I tried to induce my horse to go, but he could not. Tears of helpless rage at this trick fate had played me ran unheeded down my cheeks as I tried to think of a way to reach Dick. I saw Lizzie running toward me. Then I realized I had been crying and was ashamed. "Don't dare think I cried because I am afraid," I said. She said, "No, No, No, but run, please do, Johnnie." I carried a dirk knife. I drew it out, swung open the stable door, and with tears streaming down my face, I cut my beautiful saddle and bridle to pieces. I thought of killing the horse that I loved so well, that no Yankee might ever ride him again, but I had not the heart to do it. Lizzie kept saying, "Oh, the square is filled with soldiers, do please go, Johnnie." I walked down the staked and ridered fence of the horse lot to where the bushes grew rank and thick. I parted them, and turning I saw Lizzie standing where I had left her. I threw a kiss to her, my first little sweetheart.

That was the last time I ever saw her.

ALONE

The Lancers never stopped until they reached the main command, a few miles from Lebanon. My cousin Dudley Wickersham was Colonel of the 10th Ill. Cavalry. He immediately, on receiving the reports of the frightened pickets, ordered an advance, supported by infantry, to repel the supposed advance of Price's Army.[10]

The Cavalry, supported by infantry and artillery, surrounded the town and, closing in on all sides, instigated a thorough search for the supposed rebel command. The endeavor proved fruitless, and they finally desisted. Cousin Dudley, after stationing a strong guard, turned his horse and rode toward the home of his Cousin, my sister Sarah. The sight of him made her almost hysterical. "Oh, Cousin Dud," she cried, "You won't have him shot. Oh, please don't." "Why Cousin Sarah, what are you talking about?" "Why, little brother Johnnie, of course." "What about little Johnnie?" he asked. "Why it was only he and Brother Dick that fired on your pickets." "Do you mean to tell me they were the only rebels in town?" he asked. At her reply he was convulsed with laughter, saying the company of Lancers would never hear the last of being run out of town by a man and a boy. He stayed to dinner and quieted Sister Sarah's fears by promising to bring me back on the horn of his saddle. This incident was one of the Colonel's famous war stories.

I knew every foot of that section of country and was not afraid of being caught. But Oh, Dick, Dick! what would he think! kept passing through my brain. I knew he would not leave me, knew he was waiting and hunting somewhere for me. I thought of all the kind things he had said to me on our long ride. He had even called me "old pardner" and talked to me some times as if I really were a man. The memories of his companionship were the sweetest I had ever known.

Since early morning I had heedlessly roamed through scrub oaks and thick hazel brush close to Lebanon, hoping to find Dick. I saw two small scouting parties of the Yankee Cavalry. I remember I prayed to come across one, yes, even two of them, that I might fight them for their horses, and in my boyish mind, I planned when we met to shoot high so I would not hit the horse. I sat down and held a council of war with myself.

COUNCIL OF WAR

The council decided that I would change my course and go direct to the father of Lieutenant Joe Crawford, who lived about six miles from Lebanon. I reached there about 9 o'clock and told my story. They gave me a hearty welcome and a fine dinner, and while one of them went to the brush for a horse, the women folks prepared me an abundance of grub, a blanket and a Federal overcoat. The horse proved to be a fine young sorrel of good blood. How I rejoiced as they led him prancing up to the door. The women all kissed me with tears in their eyes, and I rode away into the darkness. I kept saying over and over again, "Dick, Dick, what will you think of me?" After I had ridden a mile or more, I shouted "Dick, Dick," at the top of my voice, hoping he might hear me. I kept my course by the stars, which were but dimly shining, and turned in the direction of the Springfield road. Dick, in my opinion, was the greatest of scouts, and from him I had learned much. How I longed to do something really wonderful. Again and again I would imitate him; get off my horse, and put my ear to the ground. Dick said a scout could never succeed without using great caution. When I was within a mile and half of the Springfield road, I distinctly heard Cavalry passing. I got on my horse and rode to a skirt of timber on the hillside. I walked through the small timber until I reached a point within a quarter of a mile of the road, where I tied my horse and crept nearer. I found it was a large command. Clouds had gathered, and it was quite dark. I thought of my Federal coat and wondered if I could beat Dick and learn more than he could. The boy in me came to the top again. I could scarcely keep from shouting aloud.

RIDING WITH THE TENTH ILLINOIS CAVALRY

As a daredevil plan popped into my mind, I ran most of the way back to my horse and rode within a short distance of the road. Watching my chance, I fell in with the Federal Cavalry. They were too tired and sleepy to notice me. A man lit his pipe, and by the flash from the match, I saw it was the Tenth Illinois Cavalry. Then your Grandfather had one of the close calls of his life. The great surprise caught me off my guard, and in a youthful voice I shouted, "Tenth Illinois Cavalry!" It was the regiment commanded by my dearest cousin, Colonel Dudley Wickersham. He had once given me a fine saddle and bridle for my horsemanship, and I loved him. Putting spurs to my horse I galloped away in the darkness, which kept them from questioning me. I was between two fires. I wanted to ride up and tell the Colonel for I felt guilty of spying upon him. But the blue overcoat I wore brought me back to a realization of my situation. I was a spy and, if caught, would be shot. Dick had said "caution." I rode many miles with them, listening to the conversation of the men, and I learned there was no army back of them. They were only trying to locate Price.

Day was breaking and it was getting lighter, but I had no difficulty in riding into the brush by the roadside and escaping. I was very happy. I rode several miles from the road, tied my horse out to grass, ate from the bountiful "grub," wrapped myself in a blanket, with my saddle for a pillow, and slept only as a boy can. I did not wake until past noon, very sore and still sleepy. I washed in a little creek, ate my breakfast with the appetite of a boy, and held another council of war. The question was whether I should ride like Paul Revere direct to General Price with my news or wait and try to find Dick. I felt sure he was somewhere around watching the cavalry. I was so happy, for I was certain I had more news than he. I saddled up. The "council" decided to take chances and start for General Price.

MEETING DICK

I rode all that day, and toward evening I saw a lone horseman. If it was Dick he would know the report of my pistol, for it sounded like a young cannon. I fired. Waiting in suspense, seemingly for minutes, to my joy I saw the smoke of two discharges as Dick wheeled his horse and started toward me. I cried in his arms so long I couldn't tell him a thing. I think Dick cried too, but in the after years he would never acknowledge it.

REPORTING TO GENERAL PRICE

We had eaten our supper, and our horses were resting while feasting on the prairie grass. Dick made out his report, and I started for General Price's headquarters more than a hundred miles away.[11] About ten o'clock the second morning I rode into camp. Headquarters Guards saluted and held my horse. I was so tired and sore I would have fallen had not a soldier almost carried me to General Price. My friend Colonel Emmett McDonald happened to be there, and while my body was exhausted, my tongue was not affected. They made me repeat the story over and over again. I know I cried when I told of leaving my horse. Then I was put to bed, but before going I insisted on tending my horse. General Price said that he would personally see that he had every attention.

THE FIRST TIME I HEARD "DIXIE"

We stayed in camp quite a long while, when one day there came word to prepare three days' cooked rations and get ready to move. There was joy in camp. We started on the march. This was the first time I had heard "Dixie." The Headquarters Band had just learned it. How we all yelled! Ever after, during the bloody years to follow, when that great war tune was played the army yelled as though they had never before heard it. On the weary marches, I remember how it rested tired legs and made well the sore feet. I have seen the battle line waver, but when the band would start "Dixie," spontaneous yells would swell the ranks. It made heros of the men, and I have always thought of the thousands of brave and gallant soldiers it has led to death.

The "Star Spangled Banner," "Maryland, My Maryland," and all the other songs of both North and South combined cannot fill an army with such enthusiasm as our dear sweet old "Dixie." To this day it thrills me to the very core of my being.

OUR RETURN TO SPRINGFIELD, MISSOURI

We were on the march and learned we were going back to Springfield. We yelled and shouted. I remember the loving welcome the people gave us. General Price was a very large man and, except in emergencies, rode in a carriage. I usually rode with him while an orderly led my horse. Colonel Emmett McDonald gave me a new suit of clothes, more gay than the ones given me by Colonel Green, and I tell you, my boy, I felt quite proud. General Price was a great hero and the idol not only of the army but of all the people as well.

KISSES

History tells us, from the beginning, of woman's love for heroes and her desire to express that love in kisses. You remember how they ruined the reputation of Captain Hobson.[12] General Price was wiser, and when they gathered around the carriage and tried to kiss him, he stood me in the carriage door and said, "Kiss Captain Johnnie,"—and in those days there was scarcely a woman in Springfield that had not, by proxy, kissed General Price. I grew to like it, and its flavor still lasts. Every afternoon General Price rode in his carriage. I accompanied him, and the performance was repeated.[13]

MY COMMAND

We were all still Missouri State Troops. You have the paper, "The Springfield Army Argus," of that date in the ivory frame, containing the order of General Price for all boys in the army under sixteen years of age to report to Captain Johnnie Wickersham, to be organized into a company.[14] You would have been interested to see them, day after day, just as soon as they received the orders (for they were read to each division) flock to an old school house that was given me for company headquarters. They surely were a tough lot, many of them St. Louis boys. I think, like myself, all had run away from home and joined the army. General McBride and Colonels Green and McDonald took a great interest in the company. They drilled me and helped drill the boys.[15]

The question of arms was a serious one. Our army was now fairly well armed, largely with those captured from the enemy, but we had many useless small-bore squirrel rifles. General Price's armories were the different blacksmith's shops in town. My two colonels agreed to take charge of the arming of my company. Selecting eighty-two old cap rifles from the hundreds on hand of similar design and make, they sent them to a shop, detailed blacksmith and machinist, and had the barrels cut off to uniform short length and rebored or drilled them to the same caliber. Then they were polished, and with bullet moulds and powder horns they were turned over to my company.

In the meantime the ladies sewing society of Springfield had made uniforms for the entire company. By the time the clothes and guns were ready, thanks to my friends, the company was well drilled. We had a drum and fife corps of five but no bass drum, to our great sorrow. How those little rascals could play!

THE REVIEW

How can a civilian understand or appreciate anything of the pride and joy that was in all our hearts as we marched that bright, sunny, wintry Sunday morning to be reviewed by all our Generals' officers. Thousands of men and all the ladies of town were in the Public Square. General Price, in our estimation, was not as great a man as the least of us.

There were no other troops on parade, but housetops and porches were lined with men and women. The boys, under strict orders, were told before starting what was expected of them. When we reached the edge of the Square the drum corps struck up "Dixie." The thousands yelled, but we heard them not. We did not see the waving of handkerchiefs—eyes "twenty paces to the front" they maintained. I drew my pearl-handed sword as I thought a gladiator would draw it. "Hep, Hep, Hep" in perfect accord to the music, and like old troopers, with heads erect they marched. Reaching the centre of the Square, with "Company Front," we marched in perfect line to General Price's carriage. He was standing outside bareheaded. "Halt, Present Arms." I saluted. He waved his hand. We drilled for half an hour and marched back to the school house, but before we reached it, the ranks were broken, every boy talking and bragging, and no power on earth could have controlled them.

LITTLE THIEVES

That night, as on almost every previous night, we had fried chicken. They knew every roost in the country. Young pigs were their delight, and we always had more and a greater variety to eat than General Price. The boys were known as the biggest bunch of thieves in the army, and the soldiers laughed at their deviltry. I counted them each night as they lay rolled in their blankets on the school benches. One roll looked suspicious, so I kicked it and found it was a big roll of plunder. Next morning the guard brought the boy to me. I said, "Joe, you were out last night stealing." With the most innocent look and laugh he said, "Why, Captain, for goodness sake, I nearly died laughing when you kicked me last night and you thought it wasn't me." They were really uncontrollable and often brought shame and sorrow to me.

MY FIRST PICKET DUTY

I was ordered to take twelve of my Company and go on picket duty six miles down the Memphis Road. I was given the countersign with orders to let no one pass without it. About twelve o'clock I saw a great cloud of dust on the road, then saw many men, horses, and artillery approaching. I sent two of the boys back to report and ask for orders. The men wore uniforms with gold braid that glistened in the sunlight. I surely was troubled. The boys said, "Captain, let's fight them." On they came. The ten of us were in perfect line across the road and, at my orders, guns cocked and at their shoulders. An army officer dressed similar to Fremont's body guards rode in front.

In a voice I tried to make big and strong I cried, "Halt." He kept coming. I yelled, "If you pass that scrub oak I'll fire." He shouted, "I am General Hale of the confederate army." "Dismount, and give the countersign," I said. "I don't know it," he replied. His command halted. He and another officer gave their horses to an orderly and advanced. When he came within ten paces of me I said, "Halt." He said, "What is the meaning of this damned foolishness?" He commenced to swear in a very loud voice. I said, "Halt; profanity is against the army regulations, and if you don't quit it I'll fire." He said, "Say, have those damned kids uncocked their guns?" I told the boys not [*sic*] to uncock their guns but not to take them from their shoulders. He seemed much relieved and said he would order his command to charge us. I said, "If you move out of your tracks or give any command, I will kill you." He looked into my eyes and cursed those "little devils." I knew they would fire, and they believed I would give the command. At this point Colonel Emmett McDonald, who had met my two boys, came galloping up. He told me to let them pass. This little incident created quite a furor in the army. General Hale felt greatly insulted and swore he would have me cashiered. He was a very ostentatious, pompous, and dictatorial man. He had been to West Point and looked down on the officers in the army as mere civilians who knew nothing of the manly art of warfare. He knew this incident was the campfire talk of the army. Later, to his sorrow, I met him under quite different circumstances.[16]

LEAVING SPRINGFIELD

Again the army moved, but this time in retreat. The federals were coming in force. As General Price did not wish to risk a battle with only Missouri State Troops, we started for the Ozark Mountains in Arkansas. Every night I could see roasting on our company's campfires a calf, pig, or sheep, or something that did not come from our commissary stores. The enemy was close after us, and we had several rear-guard skirmishes.

Our regiment was the rear-guard. Brother Jim was Lieutenant of Company E.[17] A brave cavalry charge penetrated our line and sabered some of our men. They paid very dearly for their rashness. We formed a junction with the Arkansas troops and some five thousand Indians under General McIntosh.[18] General Van Dorn had been sent from Virginia and assumed command of the combined forces, and after much drilling, preparation, and delay, we started north.[19] General McIntosh, a tall, long-haired man, whom I think was part Cherokee, had command of the Indians. They certainly were a great sight to our men. They wore many-colored blankets and feathers and rode the poorest and thinnest ponies I had ever seen. I remember how we all talked of them and of what great things they would do when we met the enemy.

General Hale was placed in command of our brigade. Colonel Colton Green was commander of our regiment. I wish, my boy, I could draw a picture of my ideal soldier, Colonel Emmett McDonald of the Artillery. He was my ideal of a soldier. His long black hair reached to his shoulders, and his skin was as fair and fresh as a girl's. I remember he was not a preacher, but he used a preacher's privilege of using the Master's name. My company of boys was assigned as support to his battery. We also had in our brigade and under command of General Hale a battery consisting of 6 6-lb. and 2 12-lb. Howitzers with men in uniform and gold braid. All of our artillery in those days was smooth bore and similar to the guns you see now in the parks. They would be useless in this age of modern warfare, but in that bloody conflict they brought death and desolation.

ADVANCING ON SEIGEL AT CASSVILLE, ARKANSAS

We marched several days and learned the enemy's forces were divided. By forced march all night we surprised the troops under General Seigel's command at daylight. We captured their camp equipage and much plunder. They retreated for the main body many miles away at Pea Ridge. Colonel Colton Green commanded the infantry in the advance. The running fight occurred along the road that followed a small creek in a wide valley with a high range of hills on either side. Our flanks were covered with Indians riding in single file on the crest of the hills. The creek and the road were very crooked and winding, and behind every bend, where the small trees grew thick, the enemy's guns poured grape and canister shot into our ranks.

At each assault our battery wheeled into line, unlimbered, and returned the fire. Ours seemed the better gunmen. At one place we counted sixteen dead and many wounded from our fire: We literally ran after them. The day was very warm, and but few had canteens. How plain is the picture of the men lying down and drinking the muddy water. During the artillery fire not an Indian could be seen. They had disappeared over the ridge, proving entirely useless as they could not stand "big guns" as they called them. Their squirrel rifles were of short range, and some of them were wounded more than a mile away by Federal minnie balls. They were really not in action at all. Two of my boys were killed and three wounded in this running fight.

Through the thick smoke I saw an officer force his horse to the front with orders for Colonel McDonald. In the act of saluting, a cannon ball passed through the horse, severing the man's leg above the knee. Dr. Britts shouted to me for help to extricate the horse from the officer. When this was done the Doctor cut the flesh that held the almost severed limb and threw it with the high boot still on, out of the road. The bone was badly shattered. With what looked to me like a common butcher's knife, he cut the flesh back, sawed out the shattered bone, washed the wound with water from his canteen, then sewed and bandaged the stump, and in twenty minutes the man was being carried to the ambulance and we boys were running to catch up with our command.

THE BATTLE OF PEA RIDGE

I am not going to try to describe the Battle of Pea Ridge (sometimes called Elk Horn after an old tavern of that name on the top of the range).[20] The "Whys" and the "Wherefores" I knew nothing of and can tell you only of my company and the incidents which I recall. We marched all night long, up the steep hillsides, as we had left the creek road behind us; we heard firing in the valley and knew that other troops were taking our place. We had orders to make no noise. I afterwards learned that we had made a detour, and we Missourians had passed by and were on the other side of the Federal

37

army. At daybreak Colonel McDonald had planted his entire battery on a high knoll overlooking their camp. This hill or knoll was so steep that the horses were unhitched and the men aided my boys and with whispered order pulled the guns to the top. The officers' orders were in hushed voices. The first indication the enemy had of our presence was the rapid firing of McDonald's eight guns loaded with canister shot. We captured their tents, commissary, and quartermaster's stores, and had the rest of the commands been as prompt, the day would surely have been won. The Federals were veteran troops, and their officers rallied them. Again we drove them farther and farther back. The Arkansas troops on the other side of the Federal army were most unfortunate on the skirmish line, and early in the day their two leading officers were killed and the third captured; consequently they fought without system or command.[21] General Van Dorn was with us and learned too late of this unfortunate incident.

There came a lull in the fighting. I was most anxious about Brother Jim, and Colonel Colton Green's command had borne the brunt of the day's fighting. The men were dead tired after a forty-hour tramp. They lay down on the crest of the ridge that the enemy was shelling. I found Jim, his face and hands black with powder, lying down. I spoke to him, but he did not answer. I thought him dead and knelt by him, crying, "Jim, Jim, Jim." He turned over and said, "Kid, what are you crying for?" He had been fast asleep.

COLONEL EMMET MCDONALD

Night came, and both armies slept. At break of day the dogs of war turned loose along our entire front. It was a bitter fight! Our battery was posted on a ridge, and the enemy, in two lines, charged it. The boys lay flat on the ground beside every gun. We repulsed them, and they came again. How our men and horses suffered! I have always thought they would have taken a gun except for the daring of Colonel McDonald. Above the shouts of both armies (we were not much more than a hundred yards apart) and the roar of musketry and cannon, all heard his clarion voice ring out, "Advance by hand, by G—! advance by hand!" We grabbed the wheels of the guns and pushed them forward, not stopping for the firing, and poured grape, double charged into their ranks, at which they broke and fled.

Oh, how my poor boys suffered! I have a photograph on my brain that time has never effaced. One of our battery horses, with a great hole in his side from a shell, was turned loose—astride him, without saddle or bridle, was one of my poor boys trying to reach the hospital with one leg swinging loose, held only by a piece of flesh, the blood streaming. I knew afterwards that there were times when a serious wound would so shock the nervous system that for a time it deadened pain. I saw an Irishman mortally wounded, leaning against a large tree to keep from falling, loading and firing his gun. When the smoke had somewhat cleared away, McDonald found that there were no supporting troops near him. Colonel Green was a mile to our left, and we knew he was hard pressed. We had scarcely a sound horse in our battery. They were unhitching one which had been wounded in the neck close to the collar.

I AM SENT FOR ORDERS

McDonald examined it and ordered me to ride, harness and all, to find General Hale, tell him of our condition, and ask for orders. I rode back over the hill into the valley beyond and found a battery of eight guns that had not been in action. They told me General Hale, with his escort, had left and taken a certain direction. I forced my wounded horse into a run, caught up with him, saluted, told my story, and asked for orders. He ordered me to fall in behind him. I was but a boy and did not know what to do. I rode nearly a mile and could stand it no longer, so saluted again and asked for orders. He cursed me and told of the defeat of our Arkansas troops on the other side. I told him of the condition of Colonel Green. He said in less than an hour both Green and McDonald would be prisoners and ordered me to fall in. I told him if they were taken prisoners my boys would be, too, and I would be taken with them. He tried to catch my bridle rein, but I was off. How I did whip that old horse. I again passed the Memphis battery but said nothing. McDonald was still sore pressed. When I told him—well, my boy, I can't write what he said, but I never heard such an outburst of language from human lips.

ORDERED TO TAKE THE HORSES
FROM THE IDLE BATTERY

With joy I shouted, "Colonel, there is a battery over behind the hill awaiting orders. I never said a word as I came by. I know they haven't fired a shot and they have six fine horses to each gun and caisson." His eyes flashed like fire. "Take everyone of your boys and bring me four horses from every caisson and two from every gun. Tell them to throw their ammunition away and start South. If they refuse, shoot to kill. Don't you dare come back without them." The boys had heard every word the Colonel had spoken. He was their God. In their opinion he outranked Van Dorn, Price, and all the rest of the army.

The boys fell in, and at double quick we reached the battery. I had ordered them to see that not only the officers but every man was covered by their guns. There was no parlaying. I gave the captain Colonel McDonald's orders and told him what General Hale had said. As previously ordered, my detail unhitched the horses while the rest of the boys covered the men with their guns. The men did not want to die but realized the "little devils," as they were called, would obey orders. How they did curse us! A Sergeant struck at one of the boys. He was instantly killed. I reached Colonel McDonald with more than forty horses. I never shall forget the shouts with which we were received.

REPORTING TO COLONEL GREEN

I was ordered to ride like the wind to Colonel Green. "Tell him what General Hale said and that I will meet him on the hill by the two big pines."

Colonel Colton Green was medium sized, very dark, with close cropped hair, slender and as erect and straight as an arrow, a gentleman and a soldier from his toes to the crown of his head. As I see him now, standing in his stirrups, his face purple with rage, oaths in French, Italian, and Spanish flowing from his lips, "Damn him, he ordered me, at all hazards, to hold this hill"—blankety, blank, blank, etc. "Tell McDonald I'll be there in an hour." The retreat began. I met Colonel McDonald, with all his guns safe, slowly retreating but stopping to fire when the guns were loaded. The rest of the army had gone.

Colonel McDonald had lost two-thirds of his men, and the ones that were left, except in the excitement of battle, were almost useless to work the guns.[22] Our guns were muzzle loaders, with a touch hole which had to be primed with powder and lighted by the flash of a match. After each firing, the gun had to be wiped out by a swab on the end of a pole. The gunner was obliged, in order to prevent explosion, to place his thumb over the touch hole to keep air from reaching the chamber of the gun when loading. The guns grew so hot that the mens thumbs were badly burned.

RETREAT

Our retreat was most orderly. At nightfall we went into camp in the bed of an old dry stream. It was very wide and covered with flat thin rocks. There was an epidemic of measles, and almost every man in the command was a victim, and after they had washed the powder and dirt from their faces, the skin looked like raw beef.[23] Colonel McDonald and my company had failed to connect with the commissary wagons and so had nothing to eat, when lo, and behold! my old father rode into camp with two sacks of flour which he had taken from the Federal commissary that we had captured. He had learned the army was coming north and was wild to see his boys but had not been able to find us until we had gone into camp. My, but it was a feast! Some mixed the flour in water and put it on the flat thin rocks over the fire, while others cut hazel switches, wrapped the dough around one end and held it over the fire. We had no salt. After satisfying our hunger in this manner we lay down in the dry bed of the creek and were soon fast asleep.

CLOUDBURST

Perhaps it was on account of the cannonading, but that night Pea Ridge had a cloud burst, and there came on the sleeping soldiers, without warning, a deluge of water nearly four feet high. The Creek became a raging torrent, and the men were thankful to get out alive, even if they did lose some of their guns, blankets, and traps. Fortunately in those days we never undressed when we went to bed. The men (as you might suppose) were wet to the skin, but I never heard of a fatal case of measles, although we marched in our wet clothes until we reached permanent camp.

GENERAL HALE RELEASED FROM COMMAND

Two weeks later General Hale and escort came into camp. Colonels Green and McDonald had brought charges against him. Generals Price and Van Dorn had me on the witness stand, and I related the incident above mentioned. He never again held a command in the army.

3

"We Fought Each Other Like Wild Animals"

DISBANDING MY COMPANY

Now came a general reorganization of the army from state troops to regular Confederate troops. A few would not enlist.[1]

The solemnity of the oath of allegiance to the Confederate States of America greatly impressed me. This was in the early years of the war. They were more, yes, much more particular at that period than later. Any boy could join the state troops, but to be a government soldier then, one must be over the age limit. They refused for this cause to accept my company, and it was disbanded, much to the disappointment of us all. History tells us that youths make the best soldiers. The realization of danger is lacking. Ever in our front we had that picturesque, gallant soldier, Colonel Emmett McDonald. I see him now with coat off, shirt sleeve rolled above his elbow, hair hanging over his shoulders, his long sword held over his head, running from one gun to another, shouting encouragement to his men, and to my boys a perfect "dare-devil" was Colonel Emmett McDonald. With such men for their idols, do you wonder that the boys performed deeds that would cause older men to hesitate? Without a single exception they proved themselves heroes. They scattered and joined different commands, largely cavalry, and stayed in Arkansas and Missouri, while all the confederate troops were transferred east of the Mississippi River.

FLINT-LOCK MUSKETS

Before the transfer of the troops to General Joseph E. Johnson's army, some five hundred cases or big boxes containing guns that had been stored at army ports in the South were shipped to us. They had been manufactured thirty years before the war. I remember with what curiosity we watched them unload a train of these boxes and our surprise and disappointment when we found they were all flint-lock muskets with funny little bayonets and hundreds of boxes of ammunition. They, too, were antique. Each paper cartridge contained powder, ball, and three buckshot. What fun we had with them for a few days. No ramrod was needed. First bite the end of the cartridge off, prime the lock with powder, and drop the rest in the muzzle of the gun. If held perpendicular, we could hear the cartridge hit the bottom. Instructions were "never to let the muzzle of the gun drop below level," lest the load be dropped out. We rolled on the ground, and shouted with laughter to see the men trying to shoot them, both eyes shut for fear the flash in the pan would blind them. Bang! went the gun, and the target, an old barn a hundred yards away, remained untouched. But the great fun occurred when some careless or uninformed soldier let the muzzle drop a little. The cartridge had perhaps slipped half the length of the barrel with powder strung along to meet it. Chin, Chin, bang! went the gun and man lying flat on his back ten feet away, certain he was shot. Laugh! We laughed until tears ran down our cheeks. The soldier would gradually recover, sit up and look around wondering what had hit him, and seeing us all shouting with laughter would break the old gun over a stump. From what he said, you would have thought he had forgotten his home, flag, and country; in fact, everything but his God. The guns were never used.[2]

With few exceptions our army was but a body of raw recruits. A few weeks of drill and discipline made a great change. From morning until night there was no rest—drill, drill, drill. I was acting as orderly for General Price.

RAID INTO MISSOURI

Colonel Burbage and Brother Dick (who was a major now) was ordered with some six or seven hundred cavalry to make a raid into Missouri.[3] I begged General Price to let me go with them, and he consented. The object or destination of our expedition I did not know, and I did not care. We rode many miles in the seven days journey, following few roads. Our guides led us through an almost uninhabited section. We rode at will, with songs, jokes, and laughter. One afternoon we halted at a stream; orders were "unsaddle and feed, and pay particular attention to your horse's feet." Each company had its own blacksmiths. The shoes of all the horses were examined and, if loose, were renailed. After nightfall we were on our horses for a long night ride. Our direction was entirely changed. Officers rode along the line saying, "No loud talking, move as quietly as possible." We spoke only in whispers, and not one of us was then tired or sleepy. Just before morning we went into camp in a dense forest. "No foraging, leaving camp, or fires" were the orders. We then knew we were at last in the enemy's country. About ten o'clock next morning brother Dick and two scouts came riding their tired horses into camp. They talked with Colonel

Burbage quite a long time. While Brother Dick was eating his breakfast he told me, in confidence, that they had seen a very large army train. The wagon train was more than two miles long, with a heavy escort of cavalry. He was sure they would camp tonight in an old field where the main road crossed the creek, about six or seven miles from where we now were. Very quietly we saddled and followed the creek to within a mile of the ford. The command was divided and hidden in the timber. A few scouts were sent out to watch the enemy and report if they had changed their course.

I CAPTURE TWO PRISONERS

We scattered, hid our horses, and crawled in the tall prairie grass until we could see the main road. How my heart beat as I watched that long train winding its way over the crooked prairie road. I tried to count them but failed. There was a large body of cavalry in their front, squads lined either side, with the main body bringing up the rear. Had my horse not been in timber nearly a mile away, I would, out of curiosity, have slipped back to camp to learn what disposition Colonel Burbage had made of our men to surprise them. I felt sure the larger part would be dismounted.

It was the hour of sundown. Small parties of from two to ten were leaving the command to forage in every direction. I crawled back through the tall grass, as I saw two soldiers start toward a lonely cabin in my direction.

Now, my boy, if there is anything in this world I despise it is a braggart, and in relating the incidents recorded here I am not trying to impress you with the bravery of your grandfather but rather with his childish ignorance of danger. As I now look back I see a joyous, happy boy, one who never made a complaint. He laughed at the hardships and often made the old soldiers ashamed of their grumbling. Hardships had made a perfect boy, physically, of him, but he was still a boy and lacked discretion and judgment. I have torn up the pages giving the detail of the capture of the two federal soldiers I mentioned. It seemed too much like bragging. Suffice it to say that I got the drop on them first. It was just at sundown, and with their belts hanging from the horn of my saddle, I marched them three miles away to our camp.

Later, I learned that Colonel Burbage had, as I hoped, hidden his men in ambush. The great train crossed the ford; the first wagon stopped in the centre of the field, and each succeeding wagon made the circle larger and larger until they were all packed as closely together as possible. Then our men opened fire from all sides at once. It did not last long, as they soon surrendered. A detail of our men unhitched the six mules from each wagon and led them away while another detail, by hand, pushed the wagons as close as possible to each other and set them on fire.

I GET AN OVERCOAT

I, with my prisoners, was about two miles away when the firing began. I was sure we would whip them and kept my course. One of my prisoners was a boy, not much older than myself, and had it not been for the cowardice of his big companion, I would not be here writing these memories.

We galloped into the firelight. What a sight it was! The entire train of wagons loaded with quartermaster and commissary stores, with the aid of coal oil, was a mass of flames. However, that did not deter the soldiers from getting what, to them, was most valuable plunder. When I rode up with my prisoners they were pounced upon by many soldiers for their overcoats. The little fellow fought for his. Colonel Burbage rode up and asked what the trouble was. The men said, "He won't give up his overcoat." Colonel Burbage ordered him to turn it over to the men. He said, "Colonel, if I have to give it up, I want to give it to this little fellow who captured me." Colonel said, "That's right, give it to Captain Johnnie."

The prisoners were all paroled.

I WROTE A LETTER TO SISTER SARAH

This boy and I sat on the tongue of a burning wagon and talked. He said the reason he fought for his overcoat was that it was not a regular army coat but had been given him by his Father. He was happy at being paroled and of returning home. I inquired if he would go through Lebanon, Missouri. He said that was his only way, so I asked him if he would take a letter to my sister Sarah. He was very happy to do so. We found paper, and I wrote telling her all I could of the events, etc., which letter he delivered immediately on his arrival at Lebanon, and during his visit he told in detail all the incidents regarding our fight.

With several hundred mules, many of them loaded down with plunder, we had a monotonous trip back. We found the army drilling. How long we stayed I do not know.

CROSSING TO SHILOH

I do not recall incidents of especial interest until our crossing to the East side of the Mississippi River, where we joined the army of Joseph E. Johnson at Shiloh, Tennessee, and I saw in all but little of that.[4] I remember we tried to cut the Federal Army in two and that we marched through bog after bog, and arrived in time only to have a fight and see what appeared to be the entire Federal army. Later we fell back. If all the battles that we expected had matured, there would have been no one North or South left to write history.

GENERAL VAN DORN

I remember at Corinth. Except our breast works at Atlanta, Georgia, and the Federal works at Atlanta, Georgia, our works at Corinth were the most impregnable I have ever seen.[5]

It seems to me almost marvelous that time and age do not mar or blot out the imprints of a picture I saw there. As if it were only yesterday, I see standing on the head log of our works at Corinth a man who from his outline you would know to be every inch a soldier, with field glasses to his eyes, in plain view not only of sharpshooter but their big batteries of thirty-two pound Parrott gun.[6]

My boy, you know the effect the cry of a hawk has on chickens; yet that is nothing in any sense or meaning to the effect that the crying, yelling, shrieking, moaning whistle of a thirty-two pound shell has on men. Behind every tree the men were lying on the ground with the trees directly behind them and the Federal battery. Some trees had fully thirty men in perfect line behind them and even would try to duck their heads as those crying monsters whizzed by. Not so with Major General Van Dorn. He stood on that head log like a statue; not a muscle moved, and this incident made him the idol of the army. A shell plowed its way into the ground; it failed to explode. An officer and some men dug it up to see what the devilish thing looked like, they being new to us. The officer tried to unscrew the cap from the end, and it exploded. A piece of the shell cut away the calves of both his legs and killed and wounded several men. A shell struck a caisson and exploded it; when the smoke cleared there was scarcely anything left. Men, horses, and even wheels were not recognizable. Such is war; may you never know anything of it except from history.

OUR WASTING ARMY

I know we fought each other like wild animals. It made but

little difference, we can now see, in the general result, who won the victory on any special battlefield. We of the South had no men to take the place of our dead and wounded. Every able bodied man was in the ranks, and each day our army grew less and less, and its dead, wounded, and prisoners could never be replaced. The northern army, while their loss was as great as ours, had new and fresh men day by day taking the place of the dead; and instead of their army growing less as the war went on, they had a greater number in the field at its close than at any time previous. With us it was really extermination. We crossed over and went into the Battle of Shiloh an army corps; we came out of Vicksburg, a small division, then a brigade, and that gallant body of men at the close of the war mustered less than a regiment. It seems marvelous, looking back more than fifty years, that we did not realize these conditions. What influence or power compelled us to hang on, with more than bull dog tenacity, will never be known. In victory or defeat; in the long marches of both day and night, half fed, half clothed, and half shod; that gallant army, never discouraged, never complaining, never paid, fought on through those bloody years until their old battle flags had been shot into shreds; until there was no one left to defend it.

A PRAYING NATION

We were a praying nation in those days, both North and South. Each regiment had its chaplain. In almost every home, no matter how humble, how crude and plain its furnishings, there usually stood in the best room the stand or centre table, on which lay the large family Bible. The custom in almost every home in that long ago was for father or mother to read each night a chapter from that Holy Book, and kneel and pray God to spare the life of their loved ones, to stop the bloody war. "Peace, Peace, Oh God" was the cry of the Nation. God answered not their prayers. We continued to butcher each other.

SOUTHERN WOMEN

In all the histories of the world you cannot find record of braver or more gallant soldiers than those of the South. But there was a people so much braver, so much more self-sacrificing, so much nobler, that the luster of the chivalry of the soldiery of the South was dimmed by comparison. I mean the mothers of the South. Last year, Father was killed way off yonder in Virginia, and his body thrown with hundreds of others in that unmarked trench. The oldest died six months ago at Shiloh; the next boy was brought home to be a mother's loving care the rest of her sad life. She called her precious baby boy, pointed to his father's gun, and with tears streaming from her eyes said, "My son, for the honor of your father, your brothers, your country and myself, take it and go." My boy, it hurts me to write this to you, but I wish you to know what war really means. I pray God that you and none that come after you may have the experience of your grandfather.

GENERAL SHERMAN

General Sherman said, "War is Hell." He was considered a great authority in those days. I myself do not know, but if in any way hell described in the Bible is similar to our Civil War, avoid it. Don't go there. You would find it a place of ruin, desolation, and suffering.

The hell General Sherman meant was once a country of beautiful and happy homes; of a prosperous, chivalrous people and growing towns and villages; a Christian nation whose church spires dotted the entire landscape. Around the happy fire sides were children with laughter and song, as quiet and peaceful and loving as our own homes of today. Imagine a territory much larger than the State of California, with a much greater population, left desolate and ruined. Women and children fleeing in the night from their burning homes, carrying on their backs all their belongings to—they knew not where. Not a house, barn, fence was left, not a bushel of grain of any kind, and after the war the only sign of former habitation was the thousands and thousands of chimneys that would not burn.

CURIOSITY

Now, my boy, if you will go with me, for a little while at least, we will leave the rattle of musketry and roar of artillery.

I was acting aide to Brigadier General Colton Green, and by his orders I was riding at his side. We had left the army in our rear and were riding over the country, stopping at nightfall at some house or sleeping in our blankets under the stars. I had as much curiosity as you have, and was as prone to ask questions, but many times found it against the rules of the army school. "Obey orders and ask no questions" had been told me more than once. I remember there was no order harder for me to obey. Had I been a man, I think I would have spent most of my time in the guard house for this breach of discipline.

General Green, when we were alone, frequently called me "my son," and I believe he loved me. I think he enjoyed the curiosity he saw in my face, but never once did he enlighten me as to the purpose of our ride; notwithstanding it was a joyous holiday to me. After many days we came, one lovely morning, to a beautiful little river. There was a guard standing at the ferry boat, and when he examined our passports, he saluted and we ferried across in the little boat. There was a large cable or rope swung across the river, and when he shoved the boat off, the guy ropes attached by pulleys to the cable caused the current to swing our boat to the other side.

FAIRYLAND

I wish I could describe the "Fairyland" that the little boat brought us to. It seemed to us both to be Paradise, the Garden of Eden. The whole face of nature seemed changed. As we rode along that shady road we heard not the fife and drum but birds singing in the trees, shrubs, and vines that seemed the most beautiful and fragrant and green God ever created. We saw squirrels running up the trees, and just ahead, in the road, was a covey of quail [that,] with no sign of fear, gave us the right-of-way. The road had known but little service. There were no deep ruts caused by the heavy wheels of the artillery. War had not yet reached this Paradise of beauty and peace. It was like being transported from the "Hell" I have been telling you of to the Heaven I hope for. Our reins hung loose from the pommels of our saddles, our horses walked at will, nibbling the green things by the wayside. We spoke not. My mind had taken me back home; I was on my good horse out on the prairie. Suddenly General Green said, "Halt," and uncovering his head he offered the first and only prayer I ever heard him make. "Peace, Oh God, give us peace." His cheeks were wet with tears. It was the only time I ever knew him to be ashamed. He leaned over, put his hand on mine, and said, "My dear boy, never mention this."

We stopped at a spring for lunch. There was a rustic seat made from grape-vines close by which was covered and shaded by honeysuckle. Again we saddled and rode until through the well-tended trees we saw a wide and long valley, all in cotton with the negroes in their white clothes at work. Away yonder in the hills on our right were droves of sheep and cattle. The dove of peace seemed to hover over all, and yonder through that lane of tall poplars, on a knoll, stood a great white house.[7]

A SOUTHERN HOME

How it grew in proportion and beauty as we neared it. Today, I remember it as the most beautiful house I have ever seen. It looked like a white city, with its numerous negro's cabins, gin houses, barns, and out buildings, all of the same swanny white. I can see it now, with its great Corinthian columns, wide, vine-covered balconies, and the great wide massive steps leading to it.

Two negroes in livery held our horses. General Green sent in his card and credentials. Then a big, pompous butler, black as night, with many bows and curtsies, showed us into the reception room. I have been in many beautiful homes since then (have admired what we call art, refinement, and elegance of the present day), but never before, or since, has such a perfect picture of a home, true in every sense, crossed my vision. The ceilings were fully twenty feet high, frescoed by a great artist; the walls were covered with paintings in massive gold frames; the furniture, priceless old mahogany.

LITTLE MARY

We stood to meet a grand old white-haired gentleman, formerly a major in the United States Army. He had lost a leg in the war with Mexico and now stood supported by crutches. The sweetest, most beautiful, white-haired old lady, in lace cap and hoop skirt, stood by his side. They gave us a welcome that only southern people can give. Our introductions over, General Green had said flattering things of me; while he and our host were talking, the lady said, "Captain Johnnie, come stand by me." She was almost the only woman who had spoken to me since the war began, and when she put her arm around me as I stood by her, I had to fight to keep the tears back.

She called Mary, her only little girl, and introduced me to her. How plain is that picture. Mary stood on the other side, and her mother's arm was around her. They asked many questions, and as I felt free from embarrassment, talked freely. Finally we were sent upstairs to dress for dinner. A bright black negro boy was given me as my servant. I will not try to tell you of my room. It was the most beautiful one I ever had seen. The boy asked me to take off my clothes. He emptied my pockets and gave my clothes to a waiting negro. There was an old fashioned, zinc bath tub. Think of it, my boy! I do not believe I had been in a regular bath tub since we had moved from St. Louis. He scrubbed and scrubbed and scrubbed me, and at last said, "Massa Captain Johnnie, you just stay in the tub and soak, I'll be back in a minute." I learned afterwards he had gone to his Missus and told of the wretched, dilapidated condition of my underclothing. She gave him the underclothes of her baby boy who was in the army. My clothes, you should have seen them, I scarcely believed they were mine. They were not only cleaned and pressed, but the brass buttons and gold braid were burnished. My boots were cleaned and polished. I saw myself in a mirror for the first time since the war began. Joe, my black boy, brought in my red silk sash, with belt and sword. I buckled it around me, stood before the glass, while Joe danced with delight. Not only was the pearl handle of my sword cleaned, but the scabbard, brass chains and belt looked as if they were fresh from the jewelry store. I fear, my boy, had a camera caught me, as I stood, before the glass, I would have been a fine subject for "Vanity Fair."

Supper was announced. General Green met me at the head of those wonderful stairs. How I longed to straddle the bannisters and take that long, winding ride to the bottom. We were both surprised at the change in the other. He said, "Well, my little mascot, they have changed you into a dude." "General, I can return the compliment," I replied (which he did not seem to appreciate). To us, it was most surely a banquet with wine at each plate. We were barely seated when General Green remarked, "Captain Johnnie doesn't care for wine." The wine glasses were immediately removed from my place, and during the two weeks I was there it was never again at my plate. We all had big embroidered napkins. I was uncertain what to do with mine as I did so wish to be on my best behavior. Then I saw all the others tuck them under their chins, and spread them out on their breasts. I did the same. If that practical old custom were obtained today, your grandfather would not be such a regular patron of the cleaners.

I TELL MY STORIES

It was not cold, but there was a hickory fire in the great fire place in the living room. Father, mother, daughter, and guests were seated in the firelight. General Green and our host insisted upon my relating incidents of our army life. He used to have to order me to tell stories to his guests, but this night Mother asked me, little Mary pleaded, and my clothes being so clean and bright, I willingly stood up to tell my tale. Little Mary said, "Wait, please," and, turning to her parents, asked "May I call the servants?" At their consent she passed out of the door to return shortly with twelve or fourteen house servants, including my boy, Joe. How quietly they came in and squatted in a semi-circle on the floor in the background. I was asked to stand on the hearth with my back to the firelight. The candles were snuffed; little Mary was on the rug at my feet. I told many of the incidents which I have here previously related.

The mind is truly God's great photographer; only death can make their pictures fade. If an art photograph were in my hand today it would show only the bleak, dead outlines; while I have always in mind the living, perfect picture of the brightest and happiest night of my boyhood life. When we said good-night, Mother kissed me on the forehead, and I was very happy. When I went to bed Joe took my clothes and boots out of the room. Next morning as I said "Come" to his rap, he placed a silver tray with coffee and crackers on the little table by my bed. When I was dressed I found not only the holes in my pockets, but every rip and tear in my uniform neatly mended. Those were surely happy days.

IN THE FIG GROVE

Next morning little Mary said, "Come with me, Captain Johnnie, to the fig grove." We strolled through the most beautiful, picturesque gardens, and I noticed she carried a basket covered with a napkin: "Mary, let me carry the basket." She in her pretty, coquettish way, refused. "What is it?" I asked. She said, "It contains a beautiful silver platter with sugar and creamer to match, that belonged to my great grandfather." "What are you bringing it out here for?" I could not resist asking. "Have patience a little longer, and you will know." When we had reached the orchards and were among the fig trees, she said, "Gather only the ugliest, biggest, blackest ones." I brought them to her. With skillful hands, she prepared them, and from a beautiful dish, in a rustic, vineclad bower, we ate them. Could it be that only yesterday I was on the firing line?

When we reached home, Mother, Father, and General Green were sitting on the porch. Mary said, "Mother, what do you think Captain Johnnie said to me as we were eating creamed figs in the bower?" "I don't know, what did he say?" "He said, 'Mary, are you real? Are we really flesh and blood, or is this only a dream?' He frightened me and we came home." I can see that sweet, white haired mother standing there and can hear her saying, "No, my child, in your innocence you cannot appreciate that for two years he has been away from home, with men, amid the carnage of battle and roar of artillery, and on this, his first day from it, he goes with you, my child, to the quiet, peaceful bower to eat creamed figs prepared by your hands. It would be a marvel if he did not feel he was dreaming. I hope he and the General will stay with us until he can realize it is no dream." With wet eyes turned to Heaven and almost in a whisper, she said, "Oh, God, let strife, suffering, and death cease. Spare, oh spare my two sons."

COMPANY OF BOY ARTILLERY

There were no able-bodied men left in this entire section. Had there been one and he had not joined the army, he would have been tarred and feathered. But there were a lot of boys too young even for our army to accept. They had organized a company of artillery and had three breech loading, one pound guns, pretty little brass ones, really toys.

Through General Green and our host and "darkies" the boys had heard of me, and to our surprise one afternoon, the Company, with one horse drawing each gun, paraded and drilled on the lawn in front of the house. Our host and General Green made them a speech. They introduced me, and I said something, and with much boyish cheering and many hurrahs, they elected me Honorary Captain. They were anxious for a fight, so the older heads got together and planned our battle scheme.

It was some twenty miles to the Mississippi River. Ten miles farther was a great bend where the channel ran close to our side. By water it was six miles around the bend, but only two miles across the neck by land. To make my story short, the second day at daylight, you could have seen a company of thirty boys starting for the bend. The entire community was at fever heat with excitement. Every boy was loaded down with cookies, doughnuts, and goodies. Little Mary saw to it that my bag was full. The levees on either side of the river were enormous breastworks. The next morning we had dug out large flat places in them for our little guns. The barrels were just above the ground. Ammunition was carried and placed in piles beside them. We saw the smoke of a transport coming and with difficulty kept the boys from firing or crawling up and looking over the embankment. Nearer and nearer came the boat, and our excitement and nervousness grew in proportion. The boat was loaded with troops. She was in our immediate front, one hundred and fifty yards away. "Fire!" and the three guns popped and kept popping. You never saw such surprise and excitement as there was on that boat. Shouting men were running in every direction. The boat stopped, then went ahead. The soldiers got their guns and fired at us. Many of our shots went wild. We could see some of them hit the water, but not all. Then with full head of stream she passed on. More smoke was seen; we loaded and waited but not for long. "Whing, bang" came a big shell from a gunboat, and they kept coming. We pulled our little guns down from the embankment and hitched our horses. Boys, horses, and guns scampered away. We scurried the two miles across the bend, where we made ready, knowing we had beaten the transport. When she came in shore we were both prepared. Our shots were better directed, and so were theirs. Three of the boys were wounded. The shells of the gunboat followed us, so we gallantly retreated. How proud those boys were of their wounds, and when we reached home, what heroes the girls made of them, to the envy of the rest of us.

I TAKE DISPATCHES TO GENERAL KIRBY SMITH

General Green had not been well for some time and, instead of improving under our restful conditions, gradually grew worse and had to spend most of the time in bed. He and our host had long talks. One day when Mary and I were talking in our favorite retreat, Bill, the General's servant, came and said, "The General wishes to see you." I hastened to his side. "Captain Johnnie," he said. "My orders are to deliver dispatches to General Kirby Smith, west of the Mississippi River. My old wound has again broken out, and I am unable at present to attempt their delivery. Do you think, Captain Johnnie, I could trust you for their safe delivery?" I saluted and said, "Yes Sir."

It caused much sorrow in that household. The mother begged that I be not sent; told of the dangers; how the river was patrolled by not only men but gunboats as well. Still I was anxious to go. Skiffs and in fact every kind of boat on either side of the river had been destroyed. My host sent away one of his black men, and next day he brought back an old white man. He and the General had a long talk and decided I was to leave with him the following morning. General Green had given me explicit instructions to deliver the package to someone of the rank of Captain or over, in the regular army, and he would find orders for the delivery to General Kirby Smith. My instructions were to return as soon as possible, and if I got across safely I was to give the man a note to that effect. Our host was to give him a fine horse on the delivery of the note.

Little Mary and I spent most of that afternoon together.

CROSSING THE MISSISSIPPI RIVER

At sun up the next morning, I rode away. The goodbyes, blessings, and tears I shall never forget. My boy Joe cried and begged to go. Little Mary took one of my brass buttons for a keepsake. We rode all day and into the night through the river bottoms before we came to his flat-bottomed boat, hidden in the willows half a mile from the river. We spent most of the night and the next day forcing cotton into the cracks and seams of the old boat. It seemed an endless job, as it had not seen water for many months. We both thought we had stopped every crack and made her seaworthy, and the next night we started on our journey. By tying the rope to my horse's tail, we dragged it to the river. Fortunately for us we left an old tin bucket in the boat, for it proved to be our salvation.

The night was very dark, and the river two and a half miles wide. We shoved the boat into the water. I had taken the saddle and traps off my horse, as I had to take him with me, not knowing how many miles I would have to travel to find a captain to whom I could give my dispatches. The man got in and took the oars while I sat in the stern, and after much persuasion, my horse took the water. He swam even and true. I held him to the side of the boat by his bit.

When we had gone out of our little lagoon and reached the body of the river, we saw the lights of three gunboats. The man wanted to go back, but I, like a boy, would not listen to it, so we changed our course and went between the two that were farthest apart. My horse swam noiselessly, and [when] we had gone a third of the way he turned on his side and floated. I felt my feet were wet and to our horror found the boat was leaking badly. With one hand I grabbed the tin bucket and baled as never a boy baled before. I still held my horse. The man bent his back to the muffled oars, and for hours and hours, it seemed to me, we spoke never a word. The water was gainly rapidly on me. The man whispered, "You d— fool, let the horse go," but I held on and tried to work the harder. The water had reached nearly to our knees, and our speed was slower and slower. We could just distinguish in the dim light the outline of the other bank by the heavy fringe of the willow trees that lined it.

Hope had almost gone. I could not swim. The man sat facing me and suddenly whispered, "Look at your horse, what is he doing?" I did not turn but putting my hand back could feel his shoulders. I told the man so, and he said with an oath, "He's walking." I did not at first realize what it meant. The man slid out of the boat into the water, and it was barely up to his shoulders. He said, "Kid, we are all right now. I'll walk and lighten the load. You stay in or you'd drown." He walked and pulled; it was slow progress. When the water reached half way up my horse's side I crawled on his back and told the man to tie the rope to his tail. The man walked and held the boat while my good horse pulled it ashore. My dispatches were sealed in an oil-skin case, and they were the only dry things we had. We turned the boat over and hid it in the willow. The man said when it was light he would force more cotton into the cracks, and next night go back. On a piece of wet paper I wrote, "Landed safe," and signed my name. In the darkness I saddled my horse and was more than two hours finding a place on the levee where he could climb. At last I was over. About ten o'clock that day I reached a cabin occupied by an old negro woman and her children. She gave me a meal of dried pumpkin and rye coffee. Nature furnished grass for my horse.

DELIVERY OF DISPATCHES

Without incident of any special note, I rode over the country until the third night, when I saw a camp fire. Crawling up

I found they were our men under the command of Captain Todd. They gave me a warm welcome, for they were very anxious to hear news of the armies east of the river. I delivered my dispatches, for which they gave me a receipt. Captain Todd immediately forwarded them by an officer and three men. He sent a sergeant and several men with me for more than a hundred miles up the river where there was a boat used for crossing. We found a regular picket at that point whose duty it was to cross at Captain Todd's orders, men or dispatches. I was told to be ready at dark, and we crossed without incident or delay.

Older people cannot feel the same pride or joy at the consummation of an act or the fulfillment of an order as can a youth. My very heart sang with joy; although I knew I was in the enemy's country, my haversack was full and the boatman had told me what direction to take and for four days to ride only by night. I will not tire you with the details of my lonely ride. Twenty-four days after making my last crossing over the river I came to what had once been a peaceful home. It was occupied only by women—the men had all been lost in battle. I asked for my host, the Major of the Mexican War. They said his place was thirty miles distant. I was the only white person they had seen for weeks.

CASTLE BUILDING

At daylight I galloped away. What would life be without its castle building? No castles were ever so pretty and charming as those I built that day. I took the receipt out and read it over, "Signed, Todd, Captain, C.S.A." What would my General say when I saluted and presented it? I was sure the old Major would say, "Well done, my boy, well done." I know sweet, dear, beautiful Mother would kiss me on the forehead; maybe she would even put her arms around me. Little Mary—I looked down at my clothes. Oh how ragged, muddy, torn, and dirty they were! My pretty gold braid was nearly all gone. The briers and limbs had torn it off. One boot was entirely gone, and my foot was tied in rag; the other boot was not much better. Worst of all, my right pant's leg had a gap from the waist almost to the knee. I could not mend it. I wrapped it round and round with willow bark, but even this did not wholly cover the rent. I had lost my pretty hat with its gold cord. The tin soldier boy was gone. Would little Mary go with me to the bower? I knew it would make no difference to my General how I looked. When I delivered my receipt he would say, "Well done, my Boy, I am proud of you." The look in his eyes would be enough to repay me for all the hardships I had undergone and the humiliation of appearing before the Major, Mother, and little Mary in such a plight. Never was a boy so wrought up between joy and despair.

SUDDEN AWAKENING

"Halt!" came a clarion, fearful voice. Instantly the big curb threw my horse from a gallop on to his haunches. My revolver, ever ready, I held cocked in my hand. The picket knew I was alone. He had heard me coming a long way off. In my castle building I had forgotten Dick's command "caution." "Advance and give countersign," the picket cried. "I'll meet you half way," I said. As he mounted his horse I saw he was a confederate. When we advanced within speaking distance he said, "Who are you?" I was not afraid and cried, "Captain Johnnie Wickersham, special aide to General Colton Green." He shouted, "Hello, Johnnie, I've heard of you," and we rode into camp where I was conducted to the Colonel commanding. He said, "I heard of your mission, were you successful?" I handed him my receipt. He was much pleased and called in a dozen officers, introducing me to them. I remember they all took off their hats as they held my hand. While I was relating to the officers the news of the west side of the river, the Colonel was busy writing. He had previously ordered a Captain and four men to carry some dispatches. The captain saluted, and the Colonel commanded as follows: "Ride without saving your horses and deliver this paper to General Joseph E. Johnson," then turning, he said, "The little Captain got across all right." At this I jumped up and said, "No, no, you can't take my paper. I promised to give it to General Green."

MY CASTLE DESTROYED

The Colonel said, "General Green left for the army more than two weeks ago. Grant came near catching him at the Major's place." "You don't mean the Federals have taken 'Fairyland.'" "Yes," he answered, "and destroyed and burned everything that would burn. There is not a fence rail left on the place." "Oh, what became of the Major, Mother and little Mary?" I asked. "The last trip of the ferry boat, before we destroyed it, brought over a wagon containing Mother, Mary, and the dead body of the Major," he replied. "Where did they go?" I cried. "God only knows, my boy."

That night the kindly old Colonel found me lying face downward in the woods, crying my heart out for my beautiful lost Fairyland, for my gallant Major who died trying to defend his home and family; for the lovely snowy-haired Mother and little Mary, whom I never saw or heard of again. Of the events immediately following, I have not a faint recollection.

STRAY DOG

I only know I was a poor, ragged, dejected boy, lost in that army of strangers. I felt like a stray dog. All were kind to me, but my childish dreams and hopes were blasted. I wanted to reach General Colton Green. I inquired for my other dear friend, Colonel Emmet McDonald, and learned that he had died while leading a gallant charge.[8] The longing for General Green still remains unsatisfied, for I never saw him again. I had no position, no command. I simply followed the soldiers, taking but little interest in what happened. I was in the fight at Big Black River and escaped over the burning bridge.[9] We were finally driven back into Vicksburg, Mississippi, and there I found my old brigade, and once more I felt at home.

IN RAGS

The recent events and experiences had, temporarily, at least, driven all the poetry and enthusiasm from my nature. To a boy, the change was great. Heretofore I had been honored and petted; had worn good clothes, or gaudy uniform, while now I was ragged, dirty, and shoeless, with but little hope of bettering my condition. My old comrades were glad to see me, one gave me a warm welcome, but I realized perfectly that I did not have my former standing. When not on duty in ditches, we lived in caves in the ground, and as we sat around the little fire we had during the weeks we were there listening to the tales of bravery, suffering, and sacrifice of comrades and regiments, I felt not only how small in station but how small in actual deeds my life had been.

4

"I Walked with Military Bearing"

We were completely surrounded and hemmed in with no possible chance of being released or of cutting our way out. Day by day our rations grew less, and every other night we crawled to the works, and the second night following, those surviving crawled back. We were sick and starving. The picture of the men with gaunt figures, sober faces, reflected in the ghostly light of that cave fire, will never leave me. They were men whose wives and children were God only knew where. All of their earthly possessions had been taken from them; yet starving even unto death, they fought on and on without a complaint. If there was a Judas among us, we were ignorant of his presence. The enemy was mining our big fort, and every day and night we expected the explosion. It affected the nerves of the entire army. I remember any sudden, loud bombardment made the men jump and grasp their guns, for we had general order if the fort was blown up to rush to its defense. It became almost the custom for the regiments ordered to relieve the one in the fort to leave letters to loved ones and say goodbye to friends.

THE SURRENDER

That night fated orders came to us. We had so many on sick leave and wounded that it was pitiful to see those men "fall in." "No boys, if you die, I'll be with you," read the history of that fated Fourth of July 1863. The mine destroyed our works, but they failed in their desperate attempt to take them. By starvation they compelled our surrender. We had stacked our guns and were standing or lying on the ground inside our works, surely the most wretched lot of men the world has ever seen. A Federal command in their fine blue uniforms and brass buttons was marching past, or at least the Colonel tried to make them, but the men broke ranks. I remember a big private sat down beside me saying, "My God, Johnnie, I did not think it was as bad as this," as he watched me eat from his bountiful haversack.

PAROLED

We were paroled and sent to Demopolis, Alabama.[1] I was allowed to keep my little pearl handled sword, but some one stole it. The pistol you have, I was permitted to retain. At Demopolis we reorganized and, after some time, received clothing made of grey confederate cloth. I was most unfortunate with my new suit. It consisted of jacket and trousers of woolen material. In order to cleanse my suit, I, one night, placed them in a kettle of boiling water. Imagine my surprise and horror when I took them from the kettle. They had shrunk, shriveled, contracted, and closed up so that I could scarcely get an arm in the pants leg. My next suit of clothes was many sizes too large for me, and I regretted my foolish act. The army was still under parole, and we had a fine time. They gave us plenty to eat, with no work to do, and we soon recuperated and became ourselves once more. Our camp was situated in a beautiful grove of tall pines. Ector's brigade of Texans occupied one ridge, and we the other with a deep ravine between us.[2] Each gathered pine cones during the day and made them into high piles. At night we would set them afire and have a battle royal with each other with the burning cones.

OFF FOR DALTON, GEORGIA

Finally we were exchanged and were armed with New Enfield rifles. Then came drilling. We had new wagons and artillery and soon started, under General Joe Johnson, for Dalton, Georgia, where we met Sherman's advance, and had the same old thing—a fight.[3] Johnson's army was so inferior to Sherman's in numbers that we had to fight and retreat, fight and retreat all the way back to Atlanta. For six weeks through a continual rain we fought every day and fell back at night and built new works, only to find Sherman's army in our front the next morning. Our engagements were sometimes most bitter, especially at Resseca, Kennesaw Mountain, Marietta, and Ackworth.[4]

KENNESAW

At Kennesaw we held the gap between Big and Little Kennesaw. [What] General Sherman says in his memoirs, "Napoleon's idea that any given point defended by a weaker force can always be taken by the overwhelming force," is incorrect. He says he tried it at Kennesaw Gap. It depends entirely on the bravery of the smaller force. For forty hours, more than two hundred Federal guns poured their shot and shell into and through this gap until there was not a limb or sprig left.

Then as the smoke cleared away through that long wide valley
that opened in its front, two army corps could be plainly seen
in martial array, with bands and banners flying. Our force,
defending the gap, numbered three thousand two hundred
men. Our works were nature's rocks and boulders that had
rolled down the mountain sides. We lay flat behind these.
There were no commands, only "shoot."[5]

BLEDSOE'S BATTERY

On top of Kennesaw, on our right, was the famous Bledsoe
battery. During the cannonade mentioned, I was sent to Colonel Bledsoe with dispatches.[6] That morning as the men were
sitting at breakfast around their camp fire, a federal shell had
burst in, the fire killing and wounding nineteen of his men.
Bledsoe had sweet revenge by pouring grape and cannister
shot into their solid ranks. On they came, only to retreat and
come again. They were more than a mile deep, and our shots
were most fatal. Finally they gave it up and retreated. There
was not an officer or man in our command whose face was
not as black as a negro's from biting cartridges. That night
we went over the field of dead seeking arms. Brother Jim
and a big Irishman of his company found a dead Lieutenant Colonel within twenty feet of our line. Jim was nearly
barefooted, and the Colonel had on fine boots. The Irishman
insisted that they would just fit him, so pulling him astride
of a sapling, they tried to pull off the boots. When the dead
man's body made, what seemed to the Irishman, an unearthly
sound, he dropped the boot and ran. When Jim came back
with the boots he found the Irishman at prayer.

THE COOK HOUSE

Back of Kennesaw, the ground rose to quite a ridge, sloping
away on the other side four miles to Marietta, which was

the cook house of the army. During the entire six weeks we were never permitted to have a camp fire, although our clothing was soaked with the daily rains. Our cattle were driven ahead of us and lived only on what little food nature provided. We killed only those that were unable to travel. At the cook camp their carcasses were boiled and loaded in wagons and hauled to the different commands on the front, where they were dumped in piles. The commissary sergeant cut it in two pieces for the man. With it sometimes was a corn hoe cake. To illustrate how gristly and unpalatable it was, the soldiers often threw pieces that they could not eat against the trees, where it stuck. About four o'clock in the afternoon I would often run through the dropping shells to the top of the ridge back of us to watch the cook wagons start for the front through the hail of shells. There were more than a hundred two-horse wagons. The drivers stood up, big long whip in hand, waiting for the signal pistol shot. The hillside was open with no road, and such a race as they had. All of them did not get through.

BATTLE FLAG

It was much more rare to see a Confederate flag in the armies of the South than it was to see "Old Glory" in the armies of the North. The flag we loved the most was our Battle Flag, and under our army regulations, if a regiment received special mention in general order for deeds of heroism, it was entitled to sew the name of such engagement on its battle flag. For the part we played in the taking of the enemy's works at Franklin, we were permitted to attach the name "Franklin" to our flag.[7] This flag had but little left to show what its original color or decorations had been—so torn and rent was it by shot and shell and so covered by the now faded names of battles through which it had been carried with honor. In appearance it more nearly resembled an old faded patchwork quilt than a battle flag, yet we loved it.

"The Commanding General wishes to especially mention the heroic and gallant charge of the Regiment in taking the enemy's works at Franklin." The above [was] read to all that now remained of the command. We fools shouted ourselves hoarse. Then came the jealous rush among the men to furnish the letters for the new name to be added to our battle flag. "Captain, you promised I could furnish a letter next time," said one, and so on. They all considered it a great honor to furnish from the right trouser leg (as was our custom) the necessary fragment of cloth measuring about six inches. Only those not having previously furnished a letter were permitted to contest for this honor by drawing lots, and the lucky ones, with pride, fashioned the rude letters from butternut, blue, or gray. Then one man was selected to fasten the letters to the faded banner, handling that old battered rag so reverently, as they gathered its torn edges together, "Franklin" being the last and only legible name there.

ATLANTA

Finally we reached Atlanta, where each army vied with the other in building the most modern and impregnable breastworks. The engineers in charge were from the same school, "West Point," and rivalry made them use every known means of defense. When the war was over and the works of each army examined, it was a common expression among the officers that they both look as though they were built under the direction of the same officer, or at least the same school. Ours, we thought, never could be taken. Lines of "Cheval de frise," after the French designs, lined our extreme front.[8] They were made of stakes driven firmly into the ground, six to eight inches apart, at an angle of forty-five degrees, with sharpened ends pointing toward the enemy. They were tied and woven together with wire (barbed wire was not known at that time). If the enemy succeeded in cutting its way through this obstruction, the ground was covered with deep pits with sharp iron spikes covering the bottom pits. The ones with no spikes were used by our pickets. Our breastworks were marvelous of strength, built in zigzag lines, so that in the event of an attack on the front of any command the enemies could be enfiladed by all our guns which could reach them. In front of the breastworks [was] a deep yawning ditch having on its crest heavy head logs so raised as to permit the men to fire between them and the earthworks. The side toward the enemy looked as though struck by lightning. They were splintered and shattered by the enemy's bullets until their sides seems made of lead. In fortification every possible contingency is provided for. If the outer works were ever taken—in some places, at least, we had as many as three lines in our rear, with underground passages and so situated that our fire would control the works taken.

LIFE IN THE TRENCHES

How long the days seemed!—we waited, hoped, and prayed that they might try and take our works by assault. The only reading matter we had was newspapers taken from the dead Federals. Their pages were divided and read by many at the same time. How wild with anger some of our boys would get over many statements contained in the Yank's papers. We lived only in the trenches. There was no drill, no duty that broke the monotony of our life, except a picket would slowly crawl at night through holes in our Cheval de frise to his pit, where by sitting down he could keep his head below the surface. The bottom of our trench was always covered with card players. I well remember a soldier shouted, "Joe Howard is shot!" Every man dropped his card on the dirty blankets. "Where is he hit?" asked one. "Just between the eyes" came the answer. "Got shot," one said as they all picked up their cards and continued playing. Had he been wounded, all would willingly have done all in their power to relieve his suffering—but dead, that was the end. Our cards came largely from the Federals. "I got a pocket knife and these things," said one of the boys, "But the Yank got scared when he knew there was going to be a fight, and threw away his cards." They prized a deck of cards above everything. To place a hat on a ram rod and let it project over our works and see it riddled with bullets was great sport and broke the wearisome monotony.

One great pleasure was our band concert each day just before sundown—it was the joy of both armies. Our band would play "Dixie" and at its close the Yanks joined with us in the applause. Then the sweet notes of the "Star Spangled Banner" would be wafted over our quiet camp. So piece after piece, in its turn, cheered the soldiers of both armies. During our concerts not a shot was fired. As the concerts grew more common, you could see the men of both armies more exposed over the head logs. I remember the big fort on our left had two guns that threw sixty-four pound shells. They only fired occasionally, as we were short of ammunition, which had to be conserved for emergencies. At the report of these guns, every man was on the lookout. With our eyes we could follow that great shell. We could see the wagons and cavalry of the enemy scatter. How we yelled as they ran to cover!

We knew we could not always protect our rear. General Sherman would not attempt to take Atlanta by assault but with his larger army was continuing his former tactics of out-flanking and cutting our communications.

OUR ASSAULT ON JUNE THE TWENTY-SECOND

President Davis insisted that General Joseph E. Johnson give battle to the overwhelming forces of General Sherman. When he refused, to our sorrow, General Hood was placed in command.[9] Almost the first order given by General Hood, on his assuming command of the army, was regarding preparations for an offensive campaign. The preparations were quietly made. Men were selected and provided with wire-cutters and sharp axes to cut the enemies' Cheval de freise. On that fated 22nd of June, like a hurricane, we tore up every obstruction in our front, passed their ditch, took their forts and breastworks, hurled General McPherson's army corps back with such rapidity and force that they became much demoralized. Major General McPherson was killed while trying to rally his men. We captured artillery, much camp equipage, and many prisoners but with our small force were unable to hold their works. We slowly retreated to our side. We lost many men, but how we did brag that we would like to see them take our works.[10]

EXCHANGE OF PRISONERS

Next the signal for a parley was shown from the Federal line. It was, an hour later, answered by Colonel Phil Howard of General Hood's staff, meeting Colonel Davidson, representing General Sherman. They met midway between our lines, each carrying a flag of truce.

Colonel Davidson, on behalf of General Sherman, proposed the exchange of prisoners. Colonel Howard said he would be most pleased to lay the offer (which was in writing) before General Hood and at noon the following day would return with the reply.

When the official functions had been complied with, Colonel Davidson cried, "Phil, God bless you, give me your hand. This is the most pleasant surprise of my life." They had been old Yale college chums. The happy memories of that long ago brought joy and happiness at this unexpected meeting. With hands still clasped, they talked of their youthful school days. "Phil," finally said Colonel Davidson, "General Sherman requested me to inquire, if opportunity permitted, if you had among your prisoners a Lieutenant Hadley of his personal staff who was reported missing." Colonel Howard replied, "Can't say positively, but remember in looking over the list of prisoners there was only one who was reported as seriously wounded, and I think his name was Hadley. I knew he was a Lieutenant and staff officer. I will ascertain and let you know tomorrow." "Please do," came the quick response, "for General Sherman has other than personal reasons for making this inquiry."

At the same place and hour the next day they met again. Colonel Howard said, "General Hood not only accepts but appreciates the kind and humane proposition of General Sherman and has given orders for all Federal prisoners in our possession to be immediately transferred under flag of truce to your army. He also handed Colonel Dalton a surgeon's report stating, "Captured, June 22, Lieutenant Richard Hadley of General Sherman's staff. Seriously wounded. Sword thrusts in breast, gun shot wounds in left shoulder and arm. Impossible in present condition to be moved."[11]

LITTLE YANKEE NANCY

"Too bad, too bad," cried Colonel Dalton. "Phil, old schoolmate and friend, the reason General Sherman and I are so interested in Lieutenant Hadley is not only because he is a prince of good fellows and a gallant officer, but the day before the battle, the sweetest little girl (only fifteen), his sister, arrived in camp to make him a visit and is now the guest of General Sherman.

"When her brother was reported missing, the misery in the eyes of that innocent child brought tears to the eyes of not only General Sherman but to an old reprobate like myself. Yesterday when I entered General Sherman's tent to make my report, Little Nancy, as we call her, was sitting on the arm of General Sherman's chair. When I told what you said, that the only seriously wounded prisoner was an officer, and you thought his name was Hadley, all color left her face. I saw her lips were bleeding, but not a tear fell. Erect she walked to the corner of the tent, and on her knees offered a prayer for her brother Dick; a prayer that for faith, confidence, and fervency, I do not believe ever before reached the throne of God. Returning to the General, she asked 'Has General Hood a little sister?' 'I do not know, Nancy,' he replied. To me she said, 'Oh, won't you please ask him if I may not go and nurse my brother Dick. Tell him please that I am only a little girl, and if he will let me, I will go on my honor.' For a moment we could say nothing. Then General Sherman spoke. 'Tell Colonel Phil Howard every word that has been spoken here. Ask him in my name to report it to General Hood. If he can grant little Nancy's request, General Sherman will never forget it.'"

Colonel Howard replied, "The picture of that scene in General Sherman's tent, with every word just as you have spoken, are indelibly printed on my memory. Word for word, it will be told to General Hood. If it affects him as it has me, and he feels that it is not impossible, he most surely will grant it. If he grants your request, the battle flag on the fort at our left will dip three times at noon tomorrow. At three o'clock an officer with white flag will meet her on this spot." Continuing, he said, "I feel it would be unnecessary for me to say, if she comes, she will be treated with the same courtesy a Southern soldier always pays to womanhood."

MY NEW DUTIES

I, of course, at this time knew nothing of the above incident. At noon a soldier shouted, "Something going to happen! Look at them dipping the flag on the big fort!" Our excitement grew more intense when an officer came down our trench shouting, "Captain Johnnie Wickersham." "Here," I cried. The major took me to one side and said, "Captain, General Hood has selected you, as the youngest commissioned officer in the army, to escort a little Yankee girl whom you, with a flag of truce, will meet at exactly three o'clock on the spot where the exchange of prisoners took place. You are to conduct her to the General Hospital, where her brother is seriously wounded. Until further orders, you are released from your present duties and will be held responsible for the care and comfort of Lieutenant Hadley of General Sherman's staff and his little Yankee sister. General Hood desires every courtesy possible shown them." Then looking me over with laughter in his eyes, said, "I would suggest, Captain, you borrow or steal some better clothes," and with a laugh took from his pocket a little package. Giving it to me, he said, "I think without the use of this you will not make a very favorable impression on the little Yankee." I went back to the boys and sat down in the dirt of that trench. "What's up? Tell us about it!" they shouted. I was so amazed and surprised I could scarcely gather my wits together. Then word for word, I repeated my orders. "Well I'll be gol-darned, if you don't have more good things come your way, and only a kid at that." "Say boys," said another, "our little Captain is going to turn into a Don Juan." "I'll bet all the 'confed' I've got they fall in love with each other."

THE CAKE OF SOAP

"What did the Major give you?" said one. It was still in my hands, forgotten. When I unwrapped it, a cake of soap fell out. You never heard such laughter. Not one of us had seen soap in many months. "Give me a bite," said Bill Havens, "been so long since I have seen any, have forgotten the taste." Big Joe Hawkins, lying flat on his back in the dirt smoking his corncob pipe and looking at his much prized captured old watch said, "Captain, what time was you to meet the Yank?" "Three o'clock," I replied. "It only lacks twelve minutes of two—you've got to hustle, and so have we. Boys, we can't send our little Captain out to meet the beautiful Yank in them clothes—we've just got to hustle and go through the camp and borrow, or as the Major said, steal, glad rags and make a dude of him." With a camp kettle of water, I stood while three of the boys washed me. How good it did feel to be thoroughly clean. "Quit your fussing, I'm going to wash these here ears just as mother used to wash mine—that means clean," said Joe Davis.

The boys had gone through the trenches telling the story. It broke the monotony of the camp. Almost every officer and man donated something for my apparel or ornamentation. The great difficulty was, I was so little and the clothes so large. They brought clothing almost sufficient for a company, and the works seemed practically deserted. Women never took more pleasure in dressing a bride than those men had in trying on their different offerings. When they tied my borrowed sash—adjusted my sword and hat, I saw shame in place of laughter in the faces of the men, that they had to send me to meet a lady in such ill-fitting and outland-ish clothes; they had no others. One of them said, "Boys, from a distance, he will look fine." My time was up. Almost the entire command followed me past the fort to the point opposite the exchange place. We were surprised that firing ceased in our vicinity. One by one, men exposed themselves, but no shots came from our side. Then the men from both armies, as with a seemingly general understanding, came more into the open.

THE MEETING

"Five minutes of three," a commanding officer said. "Go." With a white flag I started. Immediately from the federal works a little girl emerged holding aloft a flag similar to mine. Close behind her came a black man carrying quite a large package. The officer, seeing the negro, and realizing the package was too large and heavy for me to carry, or that I at least would appear most undignified with it, ordered a soldier to discard his belt, run and take the package from the negro. I walked with military bearing, eyes "forty-five spaces to the front," but oh, how my knees trembled at the thought of meeting a girl! My feet did not keep pace with the rapid hep, hap, hep of my heart. When a hundred spaces apart—I forgot eyes "forty-five spaces to the front." As we come nearer and nearer, her beauty unfolded. With head erect, no fear in her soul, she seemed the purest, sweetest, and most lovely picture I had ever looked upon. She was scanning my face, as I was hers, and when we met, she freely extended her hand with full confidence and trust. I held it but a moment in mine, and unconsciously I bowed my head and kissed it, then from ten thousand throats, on either side of us, rang out a mighty shout, not of war, but of courtesy and gladness. When we reached our works, without a command or suggestion, every man uncovered. The Federals, seeing the respect and courtesy with which little Nancy was received, gave cheer after cheer of seeming friendship that made every man in our army not only proud but happy. Ten minutes later the big gun at the fort fired, but it bore not death; it was only a blank shot to let the men get under cover. In another ten minutes our entire front was a sheet of flame.

Little Nancy and I were out of range of the fire. I told her of my orders—that I was released from all my former duties and was held responsible for the comfort of Lieutenant Hadley and herself, that there was not a soldier in Atlanta who would not have been proud to do her bidding, also that we had not comforts nor luxuries, but everything that we had was at her command. I told her my name and said I hope in time we might become friends.

FRIENDS

She stopped, looked into my eyes with that pure, innocent look of surprise and said, "why Captain Johnnie, are we not friends already?" I could not answer her. We were but children, there being but three years difference between us. Without again speaking, we reached the hospital door. It was in a very large old stone church building and had adjoining it many large temporary frame structures. As Miss Nancy walked down that long aisle, with cots on either side filled with wounded soldiers, surprise and pleasure showed from every face.

An attendant, in answer to my inquiry for Lieutenant Hadley, directed me to one of the many small rooms that lined one entire side of the hospital. I said, "Miss Nancy, I will call later," and as she passed in, I closed the door. I then reported to the commanding surgeon, who stated he had been notified of the little Yank's coming and had been ordered to provide every possible comfort for both she and her Brother. He said there was only one pleasant room in the old Church building, and that was the one which had formerly been the minister's study and was now occupied by Colonel Holton, a convalescent. He asked me to call on the Colonel and tell him of the coming of the little Yankee girl, saying, "you will find him a true Southern gentleman, and I hope he will suggest giving the Yankee his room."

COLONEL HOLTON

I called on the Colonel, as he suggested, and related to him the events of the day, including the arrival of the little Yankee. "By gad, sir, do you mean to tell me there is a little Yankee girl that General Hood permitted to come into our line to nurse her wounded brother?" he asked. "Yes," was my reply. "Joe, you black rascal" (turning to his servant), "pack all my traps immediately and put another back log on the fire." "This, sir, is the only place fit for a lady. Present my compliments, and please notify the surgeon in charge that this room is at the disposal of the little Yank and her brother." I told the surgeon of the kindness of Colonel Holton. He laughed and said, "I knew he would do it. He is the type of man that honors womanhood above everything."

Hospital servants cleared everything out of the room, and in a short time it was comfortably furnished and supplied everything clean and needful. A neat couch was placed for Miss Nancy. I was asked to notify her of the change and tell her that she and her Brother would soon be moved to better and more comfortable quarters, and so I left to fulfill my mission.

HER WOUNDED BROTHER

"Come," came in answer to my rap at the door of their quarters. Such a picture as greeted my eyes! She was on her knees beside her wounded brother's cot. Her hood or bonnet was removed, and her glossy brown hair, parted in the middle, hung in two long, heavy braids far below her waist. Upon seeing me she instantly arose, and with both hands extended, took mine, saying, "Captain Johnnie, come and meet my brother Dick. This is he, Brother, who was so kind to me." Lieutenant Hadley in a weak voice thanked me and expressed the hope that we should be friends. I told him of the change of quarters. He appreciated the kindness of the Colonel and asked me to thank him in his name. Miss Nancy said, "Brother, just as soon as the change is made, and you are comfortable, I wish Captain Johnnie to take me to Colonel Holton's quarters that I may personally thank him."

THE MINISTER'S STUDY

With every care we moved Lieutenant Hadley to the new room. It was cheerful and pleasant, with a wood fire burning on the old-fashioned "dog irons." There were pictures on the walls and a most enchanting view from its four large windows. Miss Nancy was delighted. There was given her as her maid a neat, well-trained black girl of about her own age.

That night I returned to camp and told and retold the incidents of the day to listening ears and later took my blankets and slept that night under Lieutenant Hadley's windows. Learning of a sutler who had coffee and other things to sell—borrowed all the confederate money the boys willingly offered, and next morning paid him fifty dollars for two and one half pounds of coffee. I don't remember what I paid for the rest of the provisions, which I placed in the hands of Miss Nancy's black girl. Later I called and found that Lieutenant Hadley had passed a restless night; Miss Nancy had not closed her eyes. After receiving the thanks of both, she asked me to take her to pay her respects to Colonel Holton. He was a picture, as he stood to receive her, with that delicacy and courtesy of the true Southern gentleman. "Not only for Brother Dick but for myself, let me thank you," she said.

He took her proffered hand and kissed it. "My child," he said (laying his hand on her head), "if ever circumstances (I pray God they may never come) find you in need of a friend, promise to call on Colonel Holton." She looked into his eyes, and I saw the first glisten of a tear drop as she said, "I will." When we returned to their room, her brother insisted on her taking a walk in the fresh air.

THE OLD DISMANTLED GUN

How the soldiers uncovered as we passed by! All had heard of her and all tried to do honor to our little Yankee guest. We sat in the sunlight on an old dismounted gun and talked with the freedom of children. "Oh, Captain Johnnie, you are all so different from what I expected! Why you all act as though I belonged to royalty." I discerned she was a Methodist and very religious. She believed the Bible from cover to cover. Going back through the hospital, she several times could not resist speaking words of cheer to the poor soldiers that cast their hungry eyes on her.

THE TWENTY-THIRD PSALM

At the bedside of one who was near death's door, she stopped and placed her warm hand on his cold, damp brow. Looking at her, he asked, "Could you repeat the twenty-third psalm?" She untied the strings of her bonnet, letting it drop to the floor, and fell to her knees. With eyes that seemed as though they could pierce through any distance, even to the gates of Heaven, she repeated the psalm in a clear, sweet voice, just as the inspired prophet had written it. Not a soul in that entire building but could distinctly hear every word she uttered, and there was not a dry eye when she had concluded.

Days passed so swiftly for me. Every day I was never idle; when not waiting on her brother, she was out in the General

Hospital reading to or cheering the soldiers. Twice I found her on her knees praying God to spare a life. I saw her run to get her needle case to sew on a lost button from the shirt the man wore. Love her—everybody loved the little Yankee.

WISHED TO MEND MY CLOTHES

One day she said to me, "Captain Johnnie, when you go to bed tonight, if you will hand me your clothes through the window I will mend them for you." She did not know I never took them off when I went to bed, as I had nothing under them. I saw it caused much courage in her to make the request. I knew I was dressed like a tin soldier in most ill fitting clothes and was always ashamed in her presence, but there was none other to be had.

So I called up all the courage I had and related every incident connected with my clothes and my orders, not omitting the soap. They both laughed and cried. "Oh, you dear brave boy, and you did it all for us."

"I saw that you were embarrassed about your clothes when you tore that gold braid off and threw it behind the old gun. I racked my brain to find a reason for your wearing them, not knowing that you could get no other. Why, Captain Johnnie, didn't you tell me? I think a thousand times more of you now than if you were really dressed like a Prince Charming, since I know those old things you are compelled to wear will appear to me as made from the finest cloth and that you are dressed in the height of fashion. Isn't he, brother?" The poor wounded man leaned over saying, "Captain Johnnie, give me your hand. Oh, you southern soldiers grow every day more marvelous and wonderful to me. Naked and starved, you will fight to the last."

Hours I spent telling stories. How sweet, pure, and free were our associations. I had passed the point where my clothes embarrassed me, and we could both laugh over my grotesque figure. Her clothes were fine but very plainly made. We had grown to be chums and good fellows, and I hope we both looked forward to many pleasant days together.

One evening, and the last, the curtains were drawn to shut out the light from Lieutenant Hadley's cot.

THE PARTING

Miss Nancy and I were sitting close together on the hearth before the dying embers of the wood fire, when a rap came at the door. I opened it, and an officer handed me an official envelope. I signed for it. He saluted and left. Closing the door, I came back to the fire and took my seat by Nancy's side. "Oh, Captain Johnnie, what is it?" "I don't know," I replied. "Please, let's see, I feel that it is not good news," she said. I felt the same. "Nancy," I said, "what ever it is, remember I will always be your friend." "And I will always be yours," came the quick reply.

I tore it open and read:

Captain Johnnie Wickersham: —

Your Brig. General has sent your name for hazardous service. You are relieved from your present duties. Report at 10 AM tomorrow to Colonel Hill at General Hood's headquarters.

By order, General commanding.

Little Nancy's face was white. For minutes thus we sat without a word being spoken. Lieutenant Hadley cried out, "Have you kids gone to sleep?" Nancy drew back the curtains: took the order from my hand saying, "Brother, read and tell us what it means." "My God!" came from the cot, "haven't they men sufficient to do their hazardous work without calling on a boy?" He called me to him—took my hand, and bid me goodbye. "Nancy," he said, "please draw the curtains, and you and Captain Johnnie take a walk. I wish, if possible to sleep." In her prettiest gown, we started for the old gun under the pine tree. In lifting her upon it, her hair broke loose and as a veil of lace hung wild over shoulder and body almost to her knees.

Just then the moon, that was in the height of her glory, broke through the clouds, and with her bright rays trimmed the stones of the old church spire and the tarnished brass of the old gun with silver. We were speechless. Finally Nancy cried, "Oh, I am so afraid—don't you think you can be excused?" "Nancy," I said, "I'm ashamed of you. You don't mean what you said. Would you have me branded as a coward?" "No! No! No!" she said. "Nancy, if this order had come before I knew your brother Dick and you, I would have hailed it with joy. The only thing that makes me sad is leaving you two. Will you remember Captain Johnnie?" She replied, "Every night at nine o-clock, and every morning at seven-thirty, I will be on my knees praying our God for your safe return." "I will remember," I said.

A long while we waited in silence; then I quietly helped her down from the old gun, and we walked silently to the hospital. At the door we stopped. I took her face between my two hands and kissed her beautiful hair. I took her hand and said, "Goodbye, Nancy." "Goodbye, Captain Johnnie, and may God keep you as in the hollow of his hand," came her reply. But I did not go. Her little hand lay so trustingly in mine, I did not have the courage to let it go. We stood many minutes speechless with eyes on the ground. At last power came to me. I released her hand and ran out into the darkness.

5

"To Surrender We Knew Meant Death"

IN SHERMAN'S REAR

Others had received the same orders as myself. Imagine my surprise, when I reached the pasture some three miles from Headquarters, to find my brother Jim and twenty-three other commissioned officers from our brigade. Later I learned the commands from Texas, Louisiana, Arkansas, and Missouri were ordered each to detail for "hazardous service" twenty-five commissioned officers of the rank of captain or under, making one hundred in all.[1]

In this pasture were a lot of artillery horses that were unfit for service in harness. They were not all horses; many were mules, and all had sore necks. We were ordered to catch a horse and select a saddle and bridle from the pile. Most of the latter were blind bridles. Such a scramble as we had. I caught one of the best horses, much to the disgust of the Colonel. Not one of us had the least idea what we were expected to do, or where we were going.

At midnight we started. After leaving the main road, we took, single file, a dim bridle path that led us through a mountainous country. Colonel Hill had the reputation of being the youngest Colonel in the Confederate Army.[2] He was detailed by General Hood from his staff, was a West Pointer, and a dare-devil. We made but slow progress on account of the poor condition of our horses.

One night at camp, Colonel Hill made a speech: he told us that we were selected to perform deeds of valor; that we were now in the rear of Sherman's army; and that General Wheeler's force being too large to do what General Hood wished done, we were selected to seriously affect General Sherman's communications.

AT ACKWORTH STATION

The next night at sundown we mounted and rode, as I learned later, toward Ackworth, a station on General Sherman's line of communication.[3] It was midnight when we halted. In a whisper Colonel Hill said, "Count off." The leader started, and down the line I heard, one—two—three—four. When the count reached me I was "three" and Captain Ely was "four."[4] "Each fourth man hold horses. The rest fall in line," commanded Colonel Hill. He rode along the line and spied me with Captain Ely holding horses. He turned and said, "You go and hold the horses and let that man take your place." I told him I would see him in Hades first. He was wild with anger and started to draw his sword, but the men rebelled and said that if Captain Johnnie had been number four, he would have held the horses. Colonel Hill saw he had made a mistake and asked if I would go on picket duty. I told him I would, willingly; mounted, and he led me through the brush and said, "If I promise not to leave you, will you promise to stay here until you see, not hear them?" I replied, "I'll stay." I had no idea what the plan was, but I must have been there an hour when I heard a train coming. In my front on the hillside two hundred yards away was the enemy's camp; their dim camp fires burning all over the hillside. The train had slowed and was passing. It seemed to be an endless train of box cars. It was between me and the camp fires.

I THOUGHT GABRIEL WAS
BLOWING HIS HORN FOR ME

With the suddenness of a bursting bomb, the ground trembled and rocked, and the most unearthly, ghostly sound filled the very air I breathed. The drums of my ears ached. My poor horse was as badly scared as I. He squatted on his haunches, trembled all over, and the sweat poured from him like water. I most surely thought Gabriel had blown his horn and that my time had come. I learned afterwards that Colonel Hill had a switch, which he attached by clamps, to derail trains but had selected a poor place. There was but a slight embankment and the soil was soft, yellow clay. The engine turned upside down and by some accident it turned on full speed with the whistle valve, which was down in the mud, wide open; and no human being who never heard it can in any way imagine the unearthly noise it made. No sooner had the train stopped than the soldiers in the box cars commenced firing. Troops in the firelight on the hill were doing the same, and I, misplaced in the darkness, was between them. How I longed to go as the minnie balls whistled over me as I lay on my trembling horse's neck. When the troop passed out of the firelight coming down the hill, I could not see them in the darkness. I could see the flash of their guns only. Oh! would Colonel Hill never come?

"Captain Johnnie, are you there?" came the sweetest whisper I ever heard. "Yes," I whispered. "Come," he said. Bang—Bang—Bang—went their guns, not ten feet away. Colonel Hill got one of the bullets in the arm, and my horse, one in the neck. From nearly ten miles away we still heard that devilish, ghostly whistle.

PRIVATE SOLDIER

Our command of one hundred officers in the capacity of private soldiers was the finest and oddest body of men I have ever known; from the happy-go-lucky to the most quiet and reserved. Among them was a Lieutenant Sloan from Texas, a most quiet, dignified man, tall and gaunt, and I should think about thirty years old. No one ever knew him to laugh. The inconsistencies of human nature are exemplified in the friendship, yes, love, between him and myself. At my foolishness and chatter he would show laughter only through his eyes. He took much more than a fatherly interest in me. He helped me tend my horses, divided his grub, and saved the choice bits for me until it became a by-word in the command. We were always together; we took prisoners, but he could not force me to take their shoes or their clothes.

MY NEW YANKEE CLOTHES

One evening we started out together, he saying, "Captain Johnnie, I am going to get you some clothes tonight." After riding some miles, we tied our horses and crawled close to the railroad tracks and waited. We could see the picket walking his beat on the track. They had one every hundred yards to keep us from cutting wires and other devilment.

We lay in either side of a bridle path, waiting. Soon we saw some one coming down the path; his arms behind him. When he reached us, instantly Sloan's pistol was in his face: his hands went up. "Take his belt," Sloan whispered. Then without a sound Sloan marched him three hundred yards away. He proved to be an officer of the guard, a young second lieutenant, and not much older than myself. Sloan told him if he spoke above a whisper he would kill him but that if he obeyed orders, he would not hurt him and would turn him loose. "Captain Johnnie, don't you think his clothes will fit you? Stand beside him. Perfect," he said. "Yank, skin." He pleaded, but in vain. His boots were the finest I had seen. He stood in his underclothes. "What kind of underclothes are they?" Sloan asked. "Silk," said the foolish boy. "Johnnie," said Sloan, "did you ever wear silk underclothes?" and at my reply "No" he said, "Yank, I'm sorry, but you will have to shed." The boy begged, but to no avail. "Untie the horses," he said to me, and when we were on them he begged the Yank's pardon, and we rode away. Can you imagine the soft luxurious feel of that silk underwear after I had worn only wool rags for so long?

CHARLES AUGUSTUS EBENEZER

Lieutenant Sloan had full federal uniform; we all had later. The horse I was riding was a captured horse and a great improvement on the one I started with; but he was unable to run.

One morning when the Yanks were chasing us and my horse could not keep up with the rest, Sloan stayed with me until we got away. My horse worried him greatly. One morning we started out and turned into the main road that was lined with federal wagon trains, artillery, and soldiers. Sloan wore a soft, white confederate hat. He had wet it and stretched it over a stick until it stood up like a dance hat. The federals joked him over it as we rode along. Coming to a fine old homestead, the headquarters of some general, with long old fashioned hitching rack filled with horses, he whispered, "Here is our chance—ride slow," and as we rode up to the rack said, "Tie by the best horse and mount." It was done in a moment—with hundreds of soldiers present. He took a bay—I, a chestnut sorrel, and we quietly rode away. When we got to the brush we rode like the wind. You have heard often of this horse. Sloan named him Charles Augustus Ebenezer. He was the envy of everyone in camp. The saddle was a beauty and had holsters containing two pistols. On more than one occasion this horse saved my life.

STAMPEDE OF FEDERAL HORSES

While on a trip with Sloan, we saw a pasture with only three or four herders tending about two hundred horses. He got ten of us to go with him (we all had on federal clothes). We passed into the federal lines and rode around the herd, drew our revolvers, fired, gave the Rebel yell, and stampeded the lot.

We reached camp ten miles away with thirty-two fine horses. We had many fights, lost many men, and did untold damage to Sherman's communications. A force that could whip us, we could beat running. The greatest damage to the enemy was in our continually placing the most unique and simple device that could not be seen except upon close observation, a derailing switch, that by a simple clamp made it fast to the rails and rarely failed to throw the engine off the track. The engines, track, and rolling stock in those days could not be compared with our modern engines. The men enjoyed the danger of crawling up and placing them, although several lost their lives in this way.

THE AMBUSCADE

On this particular morning the lookout on old Ball Knob signaled, "large command of the enemy approaching Devil's Backbone Road."

If you had a relief map of our coast range of mountains adjoining the Golden Gate on the north, with Mount Tamalpias as an Old Ball Knob, you could form some idea of the topography of the country in which we were operating.[5] The only passage between two ranges of mountains was nature's unique, narrow, and crooked formation four miles in length called the "Devil's Backbone Road." It had been used by both armies as their main artery of travel for army trains and artillery. As the road bed had not been repaired in many years, the deep ruts and holes caused it to be abandoned. It was both picturesque and dangerous, for in some places if wagon or horse missed the track it would fall hundreds of feet over its perpendicular sides. At its greatest height it made a sharp bend that seemed cut from the mountain side not by nature but by man, and on one side of this narrow passage for three hundred feet its perpendicular rocky side ended in the chasm below. In places, narrow cattle trails led down its side to small valleys below.

"Mount!" shouted the colonel. Instantly every man was in the saddle and followed him, Indian fashion, up one of the mountain trails to the Devil's Backbone road, to where the shrubs and trees grew behind the bluff, where the road made the sharp curve over the chasm. We reached this point two miles ahead of the advancing federals. We numbered sixty men and were hidden in the foliage so that the advance guard twenty feet away could not see us. He cautioned us, in the charge that was to follow, to avoid the precipices and keep to our left. The advancing federals, with song and laughter, were leisurely riding along this high divide, where they could see for miles on either side, never dreaming that any force would be so foolhardy as to attack them in such a place. We heard their laughter as they turned into the bend. They were riding single file over that narrow ledge of rock. They had three hundred yards yet to come. The rattle of the sabers and jingle of their spurs sounded nearer and nearer.

"Fire!" rang out the Colonel's command. Sixty revolvers threw lead into the front ranks of the surprised and terror stricken federals. "Charge!" shouted the Colonel. In a moment we were on them. Many left their saddles at our first fire, others wheeled their horses on that narrow ledge; and in their panic, rode over or forced many of those in their rear over that awful precipice. It was terrible. Colonel Hill called us back, and we divided into three groups and scattered to meet at our rendezvous. I happened to be with the group commanded by Captain Ely.

THE DEATH RUN

After we had fed, watered, and attended to our horses, eaten our cold grub, and were lying in the shade discussing the events of the morning, our lookout reported that the federals had changed their course and were returning over the same road. "Let us follow them," said one of the men. Others joined in with "We may get a good horse or two by picking up stragglers." So with one accord, twenty of us mounted and started for their rear. Captain Ely and three men formed our advance, and we, about a mile behind, followed, all talking of the morning's ambuscade. We had traversed past that awful place where we had engaged in the morning's fight and where we could now see, from the bluff, seven dead and mangled horses stripped of saddle and bridle, on the rocks below. Their rear guard had seen our approach. The Federal commander divided his command by ordering five companies to leave the road at a mountain trail, expecting us to keep the main road so that they could get in our rear. He also ordered two men on swift horses to drop behind as stragglers.

With our guns lying carelessly across the pommels of our saddles we came to the trail where it left the hard rock road, and there saw the fresh tracks of hundreds of horses' feet.

We stopped and then and there decided that Captain Ely could not have failed to see that the Federals had left the road, and that he had taken the trail. After much discussion we turned and followed the new trail. The Federal commander was both surprised and pleased at the report of his lookouts, quickly dismounting and placing in as perfect an ambuscade as was ours in the morning, detailing a hundred of his men mounted on the swiftest horses, saying if any of them are in the saddle after our first fire to charge, and he would have sweet revenge for the morning's fight.

I was riding my beautiful Charles Augustus Ebenezer I had taken from the hitch rack at the headquarters of some Federal commander. In intelligence and affection, he was almost human. Every line of his body, the glossy silkiness of his coat, the grace and symmetry of his head and ears indicated intelligence and purity of blood. I do not believe he ever had an equal for speed or endurance.

THE AMBUSCADE

When barely a mile from the old road, a blinding flash as of lightning met us from two hundred guns. Before we, who kept our saddles, could recover, like a cyclone rushed over and by us, the hundred horsemen, I, on Charles Augustus Ebenezer, and five others who had kept their saddles wheeled and started up that mountain trail for the Devil's Backbone road.

THE BRUTE OF MAN

Perhaps one of the most singular phases of human nature is shown in a fight. You have seen how, even in a fist fight, when the blood is up, all former training vanishes and is overwhelmed by the brute force inherent in us. You remember Senator Tilden, in a speech in the Senate, said "If you prick a negro's skin, you still find the negro."[6] So it is with us. Tear from us the covering that education, religion, and peaceful living clothes us with, and you will find left only the brute. Much more does this force predominate when the struggle is for life or death. Men become mad in the frenzy and excitement of combat, and while God's name is ever on their lips, it is spoken neither in honor nor supplication.

The mad rush up that mountain side while they swarmed around us on every side, heaping oaths and curses upon us! They were delirious with it all. I threw myself flat on my horse's neck. The pace at which we were moving, together with the unevenness of the road, made our shots uncertain. By the time we reached the Devil's Backbone road, we had outdistanced most of our pursuers, many of whose horses had fallen, the rocky mountain side being strewn with horses and their riders.

To surrender we knew meant death. On we pushed, digging the rowels of our spurs into our horses' flanks. There were now but three of us left when we passed that right angle where we had lain in ambuscade for them. Captain McCoy's horse could not make the sudden turn, and the Captain and many of the pursuing Federals leaped into that cruel chasm. We were going down the road, and I saw that only Lieutenant McBride and I were left. Three Yanks, who had quite a start of us, were still ahead. Behind were quite a number, and when the road widened, one man on a magnificent horse, forcing his way to my side, thrust at me with his sword. Our only hope of safety was to reach the valley at the foot of the road. We had gone only three of the five miles. The pace was terrific. Neither Federals nor we had a shot left, and no man could have loaded at the speed we were making and over a road where every step was a pitfall. Gradually the number of the pursuers grew less and less, as from exhaustion and stumbling, their horses fell and in many instances rolled over the embankment. Perhaps there were not more than a dozen Federals now following, although to us it seemed as if there were a thousand. Then came a level stretch. Charles Augustus Ebenezer could have left them, but Lieutenant McBride's horse was showing the effects of the race. The Federal on the fine horse reached my side. How he did curse me, saying he could have killed my horse but that he spared him as he intended to own him. I made myself as small as possible, fearing to turn so as to throw my weight to his side, as the speed at which we were going was so terrific, he might lose his balance over the rough road and fall. The man made a lunge at me with his sword. I think Charles Augustus Ebenezer saw his aim, for he sprang forward, the man lost his balance, and both man and beast rolled down the mountain side. The horse of one of the three riders ahead fell, and he lay in the dust by the roadside. I looked back and there was no one in sight. "Captain Johnnie," said Lieutenant McBride, "Let us try and bluff those two bloody spalpeens ahead of us." "Shall we give the rebel yell?" I asked. "Wait until they have a chance to get away," he replied. When they reached the valley where the underbrush grew thick and rank, he shouted, "Now," "Yi, Yi, Yi," we yelled, and pushing our tired horses forward and flourishing our empty revolvers, we charged. They turned into the brush and we passed on unmolested. We soon struck the trail leading to our rendezvous, and half a mile from the old road, Lieutenant McBride's horse stumbled and fell dead. We walked the remaining mile and a half, leading Charles Augustus Ebenezer. When I passed through camp in this fashion followed by Lieutenant McBride, carrying his saddle and bridle, and the men noticed my horse's drooping head and bloody nostrils and the red blood showing through the white foam that covered his entire body where my spurs had dug into his sides, a cry of horror went up. Brother Jim began to upbraid me and I believe would have struck me had it not been for Lieutenant McBride. To abuse Charles Augustus Ebenezer was worse than a crime, for he was the pride of the command. What a change came over them when we told our story! I can see now that group of listening men with wonder in their eyes, as Lieutenant McBride, in his Irish brogue, told of that race for life. There was but one hero as he told it, and that hero was Charles Augustus Ebenezer. Never was a horse better groomed. Every hour through that night he was given a little water, and his bed made softer by the wild grass which the men pulled. Colonel Hill himself insisted upon taking his turn caring for him.

The second day, Captain Ely and one man rode into camp. His story was as follows: "We saw two soldiers at a point about where the command left the road, one walking and appearing to be endeavoring to pull his horse along, while the other man followed and also appeared to be whipping the lead horse to keep him moving. The main body of Federals, half a mile ahead, was just turning the bend. Here, we thought, was our chance, and putting spurs to our horses, charged them. Never were we more surprised when, while were yet three hundred yards distant, we saw the soldier leap to the back of that apparently exhausted horse and start off at full speed. He ran like a scared devil. This, Colonel, is my only excuse for overlooking the trail."

MOONSHINE WHISKEY

We camped one night with General Wheeler's command: we had won a wonderful reputation and had been proclaimed heroes.[7] General Wheeler invited Colonel Hill to dine with him and sent us word to report at nine o'clock next morning at his headquarters, that he wished to compliment us. In the dense pine forest in which we were was a little log cabin. The only opening was a door, and it had a clapboard roof held on by laying poles across. At the nailed door sat a guard. It excited my curiosity, and on inquiring of the guard, learned there was a barrel of "moonshine" (whiskey) which General Wheeler wished to keep from his troops. I could peep in a crack and see the barrel with a faucet in it. I told Sloan and some of the other men; told them the guard was wild to hear of our exploits, and if a bunch of boys would entertain him, I could climb in and remove the clapboards and get a canteen of whisky. All agreed. I got in all right, drew the canteen, took a taste which nearly burned my insides, and passed it up to Sloan. He tried it too, then called for more canteens; in fact all we had, and still there was whisky in the barrel. I asked for camp kettles and drew every drop into the buckets. I put the boards and poles back, called off our entertainers, and we went quietly to our camp. The rest of the men were asleep, but we awoke them and handed them a camp kettle and told them to drink. I do not remember any more until about 10 o'clock the next morning when I found myself almost drowned in the coldest water ice ever made. When I could open my eyes, I saw all the rest of the command in the same cold stream, with a thousand soldiers on the bank shouting with laughter. It took time for us all to realize it was not a dream. Everyone of us had later the details of how it all happened positively impressed on our minds.

When we failed to report at General Wheeler's headquarters, General Wheeler, Colonel Hill, with staff officers and soldiers, rode to our camp to ascertain the cause of our not complying with orders. General Wheeler could scarcely keep his horse for laughter. Colonel Hill had spent the evening extolling not only our bravery but our morals.

WE ALL HAD A BATH

Colonel Hill did not laugh. They said he turned perfectly white with rage, took it as a personal insult, asked General Wheeler for a detail, and had our helpless bodies carried to the bank of the stream, which was ten feet high, and with a one, two, three, threw us, amid shouts and laughter, into the cold water. One by one, like drowning rats, we crawled up the bank, sober. There was not a single one that had a resemblance of a hero about him.

Wheeler put his guard in irons. Hill arrested three of our men and, when brought before him in the presence of General Wheeler, threatened to drum them out of the service if they did not confess the details. They would not say one word. Others were arrested, but not one would tell. Finally I was called. I had reason to know he liked me. I started to take a chair. He said, "Stand up, you will never sit in my presence until you tell who was the guilty one." I said, "Colonel, I am sorry then, I will never sit in your presence, every man you have in the guard house is as innocent as you are." Turning to General Wheeler I remarked, "Your guard is perfectly innocent of any knowledge whatever." He replied, "Is that the word of an officer and a gentleman?" I said it was. He called an aide. "Present my apology to the guard and release him." He turned to Colonel Hill and said, "I am now not only convinced that your men are heroes, but gentlemen. You had nine officers before you, and not one would betray a comrade. Three would brave the ignominy of being drummed out of the service before they would commit a dishonorable act. I would like to grasp the hand of every man in your command." The men were released.

THE BIG FILL AT KENNESAW

Our instructions when in Sherman's rear were to avoid, if

possible, a conflict with the enemy. We were not sent to do battle. Orders read, "use every endeavor to destroy and interrupt all railroads, wire and bridge communication between General Sherman's army at Atlanta and the north."

Colonel Hill tried to obey orders. Again and again, he would shout "Run, I tell you, run. Never fight unless cornered." Had his command been composed of a regular detail of one hundred men, it would have been possible to have controlled them, but not so with his dare-devil lot. Each one seemingly vied with the other to do the most reckless thing. We were only a few in number. With more Federal cavalry continually on our trail, we were on the move. From mountain peaks, our pickets kept us informed of the enemies' movements. Our advantage was the smallness of our command. They moved against us only in large bodies. The heavy force that protected their wooden bridges (steel bridges were almost unknown in those days) made them almost free from our attack. I only remember two bridges that we destroyed, and on one occasion, we had quite a fight. We caught them unaware with our surprise charge and drove them back before they could rally.

Our detail had placed the gunpowder (dynamite was unknown) under the bridge, lighted the fuse, and then scampered away. We saw the bridge crumble and fall. General Sherman's organization was so perfect that to our great surprise, trains were passing over the bridge next day. Almost every night, details were sent to different parts of the railroad to place derailing switches. I do not think we ever failed to throw one or more trains into the ditch at each attempt.[8]

WE DRAW LOTS

We had all met at our appointed rendezvous, and just before sundown, Colonel Hill ordered the men in line, saying, "Tonight I am going to send ten men to the railroad to derail trains. I have selected the location for the placing of the ten switches some fifteen miles apart. As some of these places are so much more hazardous than others, I cannot force myself to select the men, so I have decided to have you draw lots. In this hat on slips are written the ten locations. As I pass down the line I wish every man with closed eyes, to draw a slip from the hat. Those drawing slips on which a location is written will prepare immediately to go alone to the designated place, and if possible derail a train."

Lieutenant Sloan had just drawn a blank. I was next. Now although I was ever ready at all times for any escapade, I felt my pulse quicken when I read on the slip I drew "The Big Fill at Kennesaw." Lieutenant Sloan tried to force his blank into my hand and to take mine. One who has passed over the Georgia road could not help having noticed that mighty embankment or fill was known as the longest and highest earthen fill in the entire south. For twenty years after the war, as the train passed slowly over it, one could see at the bottom, parts of an engine and hundreds of wheels and twisted iron which the fire could not destroy. When Brother Jim saw what I had drawn he said, "Johnnie, give it to me." "Not on your life," I replied. Had I permitted Brother Jim to take my place and had it become known in the command, I do not believe a man would ever have recognized or spoken to me again. It would have meant disgrace forever. We ten, who had drawn the fated slips, got busy preparing for our long night ride. I changed my clothing, and to my back was tied the derailing switch. Jim tied his much prized heavy riding gloves to my belt. They were my salvation, as my gloves were worthless before I was half way up the fill. Only one who is familiar with the tropical growth of the south can appreciate the difficulty of that undertaking. This fill or embankment was fifteen years old. Its sides were a mass of tangled shrubs and vines more impenetrable than a cane brake. The black-berry, like an octopus, had pushed its long tentacles around and through every shrub and vine, and made a barrier which no man had ever attempted to pass. General Sherman knew there was a body of men trying to destroy his communications. Hence nothing seemed to him impossible for us to attempt. For every hundred yards of track across this fill and on his entire line of communications, for that matter, one of his pickets walked their beat. In my opinion they walked it very unwisely, as each picket would march a hundred yards and meet another, then about face and march back. In this way they left exposed to attack a portion of the track when they turned to walk in opposite directions. At sundown I bid all goodbye. They seemed more impressed than I. I was only a boy and did not have the realization of danger that was given to men. Charles Augustus Ebenezer carried me many miles to the base of the fill. I selected the tallest pine tree near to which I might tie him, so that he could the more easily be found. I started with a large corn knife to cut my way to the top of the fill. Fortunately I never learned to swear, or I most surely would have given vent to my feelings. To me the climb was never monotonous. My mind was continually saying over, "What will I find at the top of the fill?" Three o'clock was the time set for the placing of all the derailing switches. I arrived where I could see the picket walking his beat. It was an hour before the time. The briers had torn my heavy clothes in shreds. I was bleeding from many scratches. How long that hour seemed! I took my watch, time and again, from my pocket. When the picket's back was turned I crawled closer and closer through the tangled mass. Now I was so close I scarcely breathed. The picket was twenty yards away: now I was lying on the track. Before he turned, my derailing switch was made fast and I fell over the bank and lay motionless, the thorns sticking seemingly into my every pore. When he again turned, I scrambled to my feet and started downward. I had lost the trail I had cut when I heard a train coming around the bend. In my excitement I had not noticed it. Horror upon horror flashed through my brain. On what side of the track did I set the switch to throw the train? For the life of me, I could not remember, but felt sure it was on my side. The thought made me fall twenty feet. I lost my knife, canteen, and all. Twice I hung suspended by the few clothes that were still left on my body. Down, down, regardless of bruises or briers, was my only thought. The train was almost to the switch. I knew it would not lodge but go the three hundred feet to the bottom. I felt there was no chance of escape, yet I actually leaped at every chance I had to get away. A crash came like a peal of loudest thunder. Again and again it continued. I felt the great iron wheels crushing me and I fainted.

It was daylight when my mind grew normal and my senses returned. I lay for some time where I fell, thinking it all over. I was in tatters and bleeding but felt no pain. From this I knew that the train had gone over the other side of the fill. Finally I found Charles Augustus Ebenezer. After many efforts, I pulled myself into the saddle. My hands refused to hold the reins, but the trusty fellow carried me safely to the camp. They took my bruised and bleeding body from his back and laid me on a blanket. It was like the home coming of the prodigal.

ORDERED BACK

An officer bearing orders from General Hood finally reached us. Colonel Hill, suffering from a recent wound, placed Captain Ely in temporary command with instructions to assemble the company. We numbered twenty-nine for duty, and with the exception of seven, all bore scars of battle. Captain Ely read to us General Hood's orders to Colonel Hill, complimenting him (Colonel Hill) on the gallantry and brilliant achievements of his command and ordering our return.

Colonel Hill then requested that his rudely constructed stretcher be placed in our front and thereupon addressed us in words both brave and sad. He spoke in detail of the events as they had occurred; told of the brave and daring deeds of both living and dead, not forgetting to mention each and every one who had shared in them. He said he would always feel that no man had been so honored as he in being the commander of a body of such fearless men and that he was confident no offense would be taken if he suggested three names for special mention when making his report to General Hood. He further stated that he would call such names and leave it to the vote of the command. The names he mentioned were Lieutenant Sloan, Lieutenant McBride, and "Our Little Captain Johnnie." The Company showed their approval of the selection by a unanimous cheer. Colonel Hill then concluded by saying that his report would contain special mention of the individual deeds of heroism of every one of his hundred men; that he had kept a diary of events and found it included the names of all those on its muster roll. He said he would ask General Hood to grant any reasonable request made by Lieutenants Sloan and McBride and Captain Johnnie.

WAR TROPHIES

Then came the hurry and scramble of gathering together our captured plunder—from caves, hollow logs, and every conceivable hiding place, the men gathered their trophies of war including pistols, swords, blankets, and articles of every description.

There were four men who were so seriously wounded that it was unwise to attempt to take them on that long journey, so with great sorrow we were compelled to leave them behind. From our storehouse we left everything possible for their comfort and maintenance.

Colonel Hill wrote a letter, which was later tacked to a tree on the "Devil's Backbone Road," asking that humane treatment be given our wounded men by the enemy. The name and rank of each was mentioned in the letter. We afterwards learned that this request had been royally granted. Both Colonel Hill and Captain Mallory were wounded, but they insisted they could keep their saddles, which they did.

However, it was not so with Lieutenant McBride, who was not able to sit up, but Lieutenant Sloan and I determined he should accompany us. By fastening two poles to the saddles of Charles Augustus Ebenezer in front and my roan horse in the rear, we made a fairly comfortable stretcher, which we lined with many layers of blankets. Colonel Hill then ordered Lieutenant Sloan and myself to take turns daily caring for the comfort of Lieutenant McBride. I would have been proud to have had you know him. He had a personality most unique and fascinating of any I have ever encountered. He was a perfect type of the young Irish daredevil. Physically, God had been most kind to him, and in his Federal Colonel's uniform, never without a flower in the lapel of his coat, he alone in our command was a "beau." He kept the camp in a continual roar of laughter with his quaint Irish stories, while in every fight instinctively we knew he was where danger was greatest. In that long ride back, never once did he utter a complaint. The third day he insisted that we let Charles Augustus Ebenezer free, saying, with a laugh, he had more sense than the two of us. This proved to be the truth, for the horse realized his responsibility and selected the best and smoothest trails.

OFF FOR ATLANTA

Indian fashion, behind our guide, we started at midnight over the mountain trails on that long ride around the Federal Army to join our army at Atlanta. I will not tire you with details of that monotonous ride. Day by day, Lieutenant Sloan and I took personal charge of Lieutenant McBride, and finally we reached the suburbs of Atlanta. It happened that day to be Lieutenant Sloan's turn to attend Lieutenant McBride, and he was ordered to push forward and place his charge in the General Hospital; we to go into camp five miles out, and there to await orders. You cannot imagine how the men grumbled and complained at the delay. They were anxious to hear from their comrades and relate the thrilling incidents of our life in the rear of Sherman's army! Not one word in ten weeks had reached us from our command. I, too, was anxious to meet my old comrades, but I believe my desire was greater to see "Little Yankee Nancy." "Captain Ely," I cried, "if you will give me permission to ride to the General Hospital, I will give you my word of honor that I will just say 'howdy' to Miss Nancy and run my horses all the way back." "Sorry, Captain Johnnie," he replied, "I'm expecting orders any minute to move, and I cannot disobey. My instructions are to hold every man in camp." Oh, the misery of those three days!

AT LAST

At last came the order—"Disband and return to your commands. Assemble the following Sunday at 10 AM at General Hood's headquarters for inspection." I waited to hear no more.

Charles Augustus Ebenezer was already saddled, and with a "Goodbye boys," I gave him rein and we were soon flying towards the General Hospital so proud and happy. My clothes were so fine, my trappings burnished, a flower in my coat. What would she say when she saw me, was the uppermost thought in my mind. I tied my horse to the old dismantled gun and entered. No one greeted me, the faces were unfamiliar. I caused comment as I walked down that long aisle, only (?) by my Federal clothes. I rapped on the door of the minister's study, but no answer came. I turned the knob and walked into an empty room. I sat on her couch—my disappointment was the greatest I had ever known. My old friend, the surgeon, came, and I was so ashamed, for he saw I had been crying. "Lieutenant Hadly," he said, "improved rapidly and four days ago was exchanged. His little sister went with him. They left many messages for you." But I could not stay there to hear them. I found my horse and slowly rode to my command. Enthusiasm and pride were lost in the realization that "Little Yankee Nancy" and I would never again see each other.

MY COMMAND

I tied my horse where the shells of the enemy could not reach him and walked down the trench until I came to my command. It was like the homecoming of the "Prodigal"; many of the men, in their joy, embraced me, but I was in a frame of mind that could not appreciate their welcome. Others who had arrived there before me had told many incidents of our raid. Older men love to magnify the deeds of a boy, and when the stories had been retold half a dozen times they were exaggerated similar to the fisherman's story regarding the size of the fish that got away. There were but nine of us returning, out of the twenty-five who had left, and when we learned of the many friends and mess-mates who were lying in the trench just back of us, we could not keep back the tears. Many of my most intimate friends were among those who had met death during our absence. The boys assured me of how they had kept their promise to see that "Little Yankee Nancy" and brother had every comfort possible while I was away—told of a soldier in an Alabama Regiment who had received a box of cakes and dainties from home, of how they had stolen the box one night and had given it to Miss Nancy's black girl; and how Miss Nancy instead of keeping the delicacies for her brother, Dick and herself, had distributed all to the sick and wounded soldiers in the hospital. "We never saw her," they said, but she asked, 'Have you heard from Captain Johnnie.'"

6

"They Stared at Me with Wondering Eyes"

LOVED ONES AT HOME

When the word reached the boys of the compliment of Colonel Hill and his promise, all cried—"Are you going to leave us?" "What do you expect?" "What do you want?" asked one. "Not a single thing," I replied. "I am perfectly happy as I am." "Say, Captain," suddenly cried one. "Wouldn't they let you off to take our mail to St. Louis?" Then it was all bedlam. All gathered around me saying, "You could do it." "Haven't heard a word from home in three years." "Home sweet home" was the thought of every man, and there was not a dry eye, as they told of their longings; those scarred, rugged veterans.

I looked into the yearning, pleading faces, and said, "Boys, I'll do it if they will let me." The men took me in their arms, while the news, like wildfire, spread through our brigade. Others came, and they acted like men bereft of reason at the hope of hearing from loved ones at home. They did not question or doubt but that I would be given permission. They organized and appointed committees, one to see that the letters were short and another to gather all the Federal money that was in camp. The money was absolutely valueless with us. Even if there was anything to sell, no southern man would take a Yankee's money for it. A committee of ten men was selected to provide me with citizen's clothes. This was the most difficult task of all, as our army at this time was in such dire straits that every male, from youth to tottering age, was in it.

MY CITIZEN'S CLOTHES

In the conscript camp they saw a handsome youth with well fitting homemade clothes, and by intrigue and falsehood, they enticed him away, blindfolding and carrying him to our trench, where he was stripped of the coveted suit of home spun and, in exchange, given old ragged garments. The boy, nearly frightened to death and still blindfolded, was conducted in a roundabout fashion before he was turned loose. When I next came to camp I had to try the stolen suit on, and although a trifle large, it was pronounced satisfactory. The boys then, instead of calling me Captain Johnnie, now shouted, "Sonnie, your mother was just here looking for you. You have better run home now and do the chores."

Almost every soldier possessed greenbacks. They kept them merely for the pretty pictures stamped on them or to gamble with. How many thousands of dollars I carried, I never knew. I did not even think of counting them. Men from other camps, hearing of my proposed mission, contributed their share to my collection.

GENERAL HOOD

Sunday morning Colonel Hill led the way to the parade ground in front of General Hood's headquarters, at the head of the band of thirty-one men, all remaining of the hundred who had left Atlanta ten weeks before. Both the staff and escort of General Hood were in confederate uniform and poorly mounted, while our uniforms were of Federal blue with much gold braid and tinsel, and our mounts, the very select of those captured during the raid. As we approached headquarters, with the band playing "Dixie," those stirring and thrilling though unfamiliar strains of music seemed to startle our horses almost into a panic, and when to this was added the Rebel yell, given by more than a thousand throats, the animals were practically uncontrollable, much to the enjoyment of the spectators. It was an odd sight to see our little command in their fine Yankee uniforms in the midst of that army of ragged and faded gray. Colonel Hill read his report, which was frequently interrupted by applause. He mentioned the personal gallantry of his men, giving in detail a history of our life in General Sherman's rear. Finally, ordering Lieutenant Sloan, Lieutenant McBride, and Captain Johnnie to ride forward, he turned to General Hood and said, "I promised these three men that, with your approval, they should be granted any request in reason. This I do by the unanimous vote of my command." Following this, he spoke in detail of the various exploits, etc. etc. General Hood made a most gracious and complimentary reply and stated that each member of the command should receive promotion. "Lieutenant McBride, what is your desire?" he asked. "General," answered the Lieutenant, "traveling in a saddle on the back of a good horse is much more to my taste than riding my two feet." "Major McBride," said the General, "the cavalry needs more just such gallant officers as you. Report in ten days to General Wheeler." "Major Sloan, what can I do for you"? "General," he replied, "my desire is to be transferred to the cavalry." "It gives me great pleasure to grant that wish," said General Hood, for I have in my hand a letter from General

Wheeler asking that I transfer to his command any and all of Colonel Hill's command so desiring."

PERMISSION

Turning to me he said, "Captain Johnnie Wickersham, what is your pleasure? What can I do for you?" "Nothing for myself," I answered, "but the men of our brigade, not having heard a word from home in years, have begged me to ask your permission to carry their letters and make inquiries of their families in St. Louis." "What," said General Hood, "do you mean you only wish permission to take the mail to St. Louis?" "Yes, Sir," I replied. He turned to our beloved Brig. General, saying, "can this boy accomplish such a thing?" "Yes," was the answer. General Hood then summoned Colonel Hill, and they engaged in conversation for some time, and when they concluded he addressed me, saying, "Captain Johnnie, do you understand, do you realize that you will have to travel many miles through Federal territory and that you are liable to be hanged as a spy if apprehended?" "General, I promised the boys I would try to do it, if you would grant permission." Finally, the General, after some hesitation, using the pommel of his saddle as a rest, wrote the order, giving me an indefinite furlough and asking assistance in my behalf of all Confederate troops. Soon after we were disbanded.

THE BANQUET

Before I started on my long journey, Colonel Hill made me the guest of honor at a dinner given by him to General Hood's staff and various officers. The banquet took place in a beautiful mansion then vacant, and around that table sat many white haired officers in Confederate uniforms. Looking back, it seem ludicrous to think of that little boy in home spun jeans occupying the place of honor at the head of the board.

At their repeated requests I gave a recital of the events of our raid, mingling the comic with the serious, not forgetting to relate, to the evident amusement of the party, how I got the moonshine whisky. The hilarity faded in the exchange of good-nights and goodbyes, and the eyes of Colonel Hill glistened as he held my hand for the last time.

My preparations for the trip north consisted in having the mail entrusted to me concealed as effectually as possible on my person, which task was confined to a tailor, who proved himself a veritable artist in this regard and systematically sewed the letters one on another, distributing the entire mail in this manner over the inner side of my undergarments, which suit, by the way, was a part of my Federal plunder. When all had been attended to, and with the goodbyes and good wishes of my comrades ringing in my ears, I mounted Charles Augustus Ebenezer and with no luggage but my trusty revolvers, rode away on my long journey toward St. Louis. I decided to endeavor to enter the Federal lines at Memphis. The distance by rail was 466 miles, but on account of the necessity of avoiding the Federal armies between those points, this distance was doubled several times before I reached Memphis. I shall not give in detail the history of this solitary journey, which had almost entirely to be made at night time, so as to avoid travelers, and over roads unknown to me with no guide but my compass. The highways I shunned for the same good reasons. It seems to me the very woods were filled with Yankee soldiers, and although I knew if caught and the mail discovered upon me I would be hanged as a spy, still I did not seem to realize the gravity and peril of my situation. After reaching Federal territory I spoke to no one with the exception of an old man, the keeper of a country store. After locating the store I watched its entrance for nearly an entire day from a safe distance behind some brush, and when I was convinced it was little patronized by the soldiers, I at last ventured to get some supplies of bacon, crackers, sardines, etc. of which I was in need. As the old store-keeper brought the packages out to me, he remarked, "Why Sonnie, you are riding the most beautiful horse I have ever seen." "Yes," I replied, "Father, who is a big officer, loaned him to me to ride here for these things."

My packages were already tied to my saddle when two soldiers rode up. I started down the road while they talked to the store-keeper but had not gone but a short distance when the soldiers started after me. By talking gently to Charles Augustus Ebenezer I managed to keep him at a walk as I was not yet certain as to their intentions. Then one of the men yelled "Halt" and fired his pistol in the air. At this my beautiful horse showed them his heels, and I was not long outdistancing them, but knowing I could not keep the road without the fear of meeting others, I made a sharp turn as soon as out of sight of my pursuers and dashed into the shelter of the brush. Dismounting, I whispered to my beloved horse, and he stood immovable until I saw them pass. Then taking an opposite direction I rode on through brush and timber. Without doubt my salvation was in a great measure due to the knowledge gained while in the raid in the rear of Sherman's army. Many were the incidents that occurred during the three weeks of lonely travel, skirting towns and camps, many times entirely at sea as to my direction, and added to this the discomfort of the almost continuous rains from the time of starting to my arrival at Memphis. While I slept, my horse's hitch rein was secured to my wrist and more than once when he heard a strange noise would awake me by putting his nose to my face, and at other times he would playfully bite my hand and enjoy my caresses. You cannot understand how we loved each other. I began to surmise that

I must be in the vicinity of Memphis but could not assure myself of this by making inquiries, so hearing army wagons passing on the road, I tied my horse to a tree and crawled to the main road, where concealed in the brush I watched and listened as the big army train passed, and at last was rewarded by hearing a driver say he would be in Memphis by the following night. I then found I had passed Memphis and was some thirty miles northeast of it.

Then new fears assailed me, and if you had seen me as I mounted and rode off just at dusk, you would have said, "There is surely the saddest boy in all the world," for I had just realized that if I continued my journey to St. Louis I should have to part, and I knew forever, with my dearly beloved Charles Augustus Ebenezer. I held a night long council of war with myself, as I knew no one with whom I could leave him, and the fact was forced upon me that I could not ride him into Memphis, for on his left shoulder was the telltale brand "U.S." I felt sure a boy dressed as I was, riding such a magnificent horse, would be compelled to prove ownership, which would result in my being jailed for horse stealing. Then came to me the greatest sorrow I thought could come to mortal and I gave way to my grief. Having decided that nothing remained for me to do but abandon the good friend who had shared my trials, I led him to a small creek where the grass was fresh and green, took off my saddle and bridle, and kissing the faithful beast I left him and ran towards the main road. Before I had covered half the distance I saw he was following me, I turned in another direction and hid behind a fallen tree hoping he could not find me, but before I had scarcely wiped away my tears, I looked up into the face of Charles Augustus Ebenezer. In the frenzy of my anguish I struck him, yes, ashamed as I am to write it, I threw rocks at him, and drove him away from me, leaving him without home, shelter, or master. I bathed my tear-stained face in the creek and walked boldly into the road along which was passing an army wagon driven by a jolly Irish fellow who shouted to me, "Get aboard, kid," and I rode all the afternoon by his side. Without direct questions, I gained some idea as to my whereabouts from his casual remark that it was nine miles from Memphis. Upon reaching Memphis I felt free and happy as a lark. The city was filled with soldiers, and I noticed many boys dressed similar to myself. I think it was the third day after my arrival that I took passage on the Steamboat "Sultanna," and notwithstanding the fact that I had probably funds sufficient to purchase the entire steamer, I was cautious enough to purchase only a deck passage to St. Louis.[1] How good the grub tasted, and how I wished the boys in the army could share such a feast with me, yet the passengers were continually grumbling. Nothing of especial interest happened on the trip, except that I remember we were four days aground, which did not dampen my spirits, for everything was new to me. How did we whip the rebels during that trip!

ST. LOUIS

Well do I remember when the boat whistled at St. Louis and how the Mate drove me back from the front end of the boat. I had no luggage of any kind, not even a pocket handkerchief, and before the boat was tied up I was ashore and climbing the cobblestones of the levee. I felt like shouting, for I knew every foot of the old city over whose streets and byways I had often ridden Father's horses. How beautiful the stores looked, clothing stores especially. I stopped in front of their inviting windows and gazed and gazed at their content, but more than all was I astonished at the unexpected sight of a horse-car. I had not seen once since Father left St. Louis. After gazing at the fascinating displays of a several clothing stores, I at last entered one and ordered the best suit of clothes in the house, together with shirt, linen collar, tie, shoes, and socks. The salesman took them all to a little dressing room and offered to assist me in dressing, but for very good reasons I refused this assistance, and when he asked me about underclothing, I said I did not need any. Well, my boy, you can't imagine the pleasure I experienced as I looked into the mirror at the dude I was transformed into. I gave the salesman a fifty dollar bill, and told him to keep the change, requesting that he have my old clothes tied up to be called for later. I immediately realized I had made a mistake in telling him to keep the change, for I saw he believed I had stolen the money, but his good judgment told him that he would lose the sale if he had me arrested. I spent the rest of the afternoon and early evening looking in the show windows and mingling with the crowd. I invested in a pocket knife, of the variety containing the picture of a woman in the rivet. As the evening advanced I made my way to the home of Henry Ashbrook, southerner and friend of my Father. My ring of the bell was answered by a negro servant of whom I inquired for Mr. Ashbrook, refusing to give my name. After some delay he came to the door and I said to him, "Don't you know me?" It took me quite a while to convince him of my identity, and when I was finally ushered into the house he said, "What in the name of Heaven are you doing here?" "I came with the mail from our brigade," I answered. "Oh!," he exclaimed, "You have letters from my boy," but I had to tell him that his son had fallen at Vicksburg.[2] The scene which followed is too sad to relate. "I have a letter from your nephew," I told him. "Give it to me," almost shrieked the wife. "The mail is fastened to my underclothing for safety and has not been removed since I left camp," I said. They understood, and I was taken to the bathroom, where the letters were ripped from their hiding place, and with the assistance of the negro and fresh garments, I felt like a civilized being once more.

I trust no one will have occasion to pass through such a night of misery as I, a boy, witnessed that night at Henry Ashbrook's. I knew every man in our command, and it devolved upon me to relate to parents, friends, or relatives incidents of camp life or to tell of how some dear one had lost an arm or a leg, etc. All that night long the faithful old negro would come and go bringing Mothers, Fathers, and friends through the alley and up the back stairs to the attic, where by the light of a coal oil lamp, I told my tales of woe, for if living, at best I could but tell them of those dear ones as gaunt, starved, and ragged, but in spite of all this, never did their lips breathe the words nor their eyes express the desire to "Give up."

These meetings continued for three days and nights until the number of callers began to cause comment, so we arranged for the delivery of my mail, and I left Mr. Ashbrook's house with many blessings and prayers for my safety.

Next door to where we had lived in St. Louis had dwelt a boy of my own age named John Bright. We had never been able to agree very well and had often settled our differences in hand to hand encounters. Wandering into a theater after leaving Mr. Ashbrook's house, I had sat through the first act, thoroughly enjoying the entertainment, when to my surprise and consternation, the same John Bright greeted me with hands extended, saying "Isn't this Johnnie Wickersham"? Quick as a flash I answered, "Never more mistaken in your life. My name is Doyle, but pleased to meet you." As my stuttering had been the cause of most of our boyish differences, I now felt the absolute necessity of hiding this defect, and succeeded. He left me and returned to the seat he had formerly occupied but repeatedly looked in my direction. I hated to leave the show, but I saw he was watching me, so I waited my opportunity and slipped out.

The following day I visited my Father's brother, Hawkins Wickersham, who was very wealthy and a strong Unionist.[3] The consternation could not have been more complete if a bomb had exploded in their midst as I entered unannounced. The family were at dinner, but Uncle gave me no welcome, only wringing his hands and begging me to leave at once, as my presence, if suspected, would place him and his family in imminent peril. Aunt Mary kissed me, and my cousin John, a boy of about the same age as myself, showed much boyish admiration for me as one who had figured in many adventures. I remained only about an hour, as Uncle kept repeating that they would take his property from him for harboring a rebel and that he knew I would be hung, etc.

BARNUM'S CIRCUS

During one of my rambles on the tenth day after my arrival in St. Louis, attired in a new and different suit to that which I bought on the first day, I ran across the two McCall girls, whose father, as I have mentioned previously, had been literally cut to pieces in the fight with Fremont's Body Guard at Springfield. They were indeed glad to see me, but after asking many questions they begged me to leave the city, informing me that some of my mail had been captured, also that John Bright had reported having seen me and that a reward of five thousand dollars was offered for my capture, dead or alive. We were just then passing the tents of Barnum's Circus, and the natural cravings of a boy to see a circus could not be resisted.[4] I told the girls I was sure no one would know me in my new suit and promised to use every endeavor to leave town that very night if they would accompany me to the circus. They finally consented, and the show proved wonderful beyond all description. Nothing I have ever seen since has in any way compared to those few hours passed under the tents of Barnum's circus; and the clown—he was the funniest man, I thought, in all the world, and I laughed at his antics as only a boy could and completely forgot, for the time, those years of battles and privations. Suddenly I felt someone pulling at my trouser leg, and a voice whispered, "Johnnie, John Bright has brought the police and soldiers here to catch you." I thought surely my girl companions would faint. I seemed to leave the joy and laughter of the previous moments miles behind me as I asked the unknown friend in lowered voice if I could not drop down and so get out under the canvas. "No," he replied, "There is a regiment of soldiers surrounding the tents." I looked into the white faces of the girls and thought of the flattering things they had said of my share in the recent events and then and there resolved that in this emergency I should not prove myself a coward, so gathering all my courage and wits together, I said, "Girls, if I am caught, you will be to blame, for your tears and white faces will give me away. Now let's all brace up. They will be looking for a scared boy and will not think to find their prey in the midst of a happy crowd." So I laughed, but this time there was no mirth in my laughter, and the pleasure and glamour of the afternoon's entertainment were gone. At last the circus was over. "Laugh, girls, laugh," I urged. "Let's mix in the thickest of the crowd." Actors they surely proved themselves, for we had to pass out through files of soldiers, but we walked so closely together, the girls talking and laughing. The privilege of writing these reminiscences today was perhaps owing to the fact that girls wore more clothes than they do now. My new suit happened to be near the same color of their dresses. I held their skirts so they completely enveloped the lower part of my body, one parasol was forced down over my drooping head, while the other flitted from side to side, completely hiding me from view. "John Bright," one girl whispered, "was there," but we did not see each other, and I passed out unnoticed. Two blocks away one of the girls fainted. I wanted to stay, but the other only repeated, "Go, Go, Go," and I left, stopping at my Uncle's for the suit of clothes which I that morning had asked Cousin John to take care of for me. There was all excitement and terror, for the soldiers had been there and ransacked every portion of the house in the hope of finding me. I lost no time in securing my bundle and was soon out on the streets making my way toward Northern St. Louis.

I PADDLE MY OWN CANOE

It was then getting dusk, and quite dark by the time I reached the river. After examining the bank carefully I discovered a boat chained and locked, and walking back up the levee I loosened some cobble stones with which I succeeded in breaking the lock. There were no oars, but in the drift I found a good piece of board and so seating myself in the boat, started to drift down the river steering to the Illinois side in order to keep out of the reflection of the city lights. After passing the city and using the board as a rudder, I swung out into the swift current, a happy singing boy, and landed at the break of day on the Illinois side where I cast my boat adrift and started off on foot. Before long I came to a little store where I stopped to purchase some eatables, and then continued my journey until I struck the railroad track, which I followed for some miles until it landed me at a small station. There I purchased a ticket for Memphis, and, after waiting some hours for a passenger train, I jumped aboard and was soon curled up in a seat and fast asleep.

MEMPHIS

I spent several days at Memphis contriving how to get through the Federal lines to our army, when one day, to my great surprise, I met Mrs. Mary Davis, wife of an officer in our brigade. She had slipped through the Federal lines to smuggle clothing to our ragged comrades, and we immediately entered into partnership. Her Aunt, who lived six miles out of town, had a Federal pass for herself, daughter, and driver, and Mary Davis had been taking the place of the daughter. She in company with her Aunt would go to town every day, wearing as few clothes as possible, and upon their return home would wear the smuggled cloth which had been made up into petticoats by Southern friends in Memphis, who acted in conjunction with them, buying the material and preparing it for them. I assumed the position of servant and acted as coachman on their frequent trips to town.

IN PRISON

Everything worked smoothly until one day a full company of Provost Guard, with company front, like dog catchers on a big scale, started out to corral every male, from sixteen up. I was captured, and with the others placed in the "bull pen" where we were informed that if we took the oath and joined the Home Guard, we should be set free. Many, having exemption papers, were set free, and most of the boys and men took the oath and went their way. I refused and was put in prison. It was a great shock to Mary Davis on learning that I was in prison, and after, in many ways, endeavoring to secure my release, she, as a last resort, appealed to a distant relative of mine named Wickhersham, a bachelor of means, and a Unionist, who, although we had never met, had heard much of me. She begged him to go and see me, which he did, not only once, but many times. He brought all the arguments that good horse sense could suggest to prove to me the South was beaten, that our armies were starving, and that our last hope was gone. "Take the oath, Johnnie," he would implore me again and again. But he might as well have argued with a stone as with that foolish, obdurate boy. We grew to like each other, however, and he was deeply interested in my stories and experiences of the war. The last time I ever saw him he took my hand in his and said, "Johnnie, I am an old man with no family, and few relations, if you will take the oath, I will this day adopt you as my son, I will love you and educate you, and make you my heir." But I only answered, "What would you think of me if I betrayed the trust of those I love?" "You would call me a deserter and would be right in doing so." I told him I would rot in prison before I would take that hated oath. That same night a bribed prison guard set me free, and before morning I was at the home of Mary Davis' Aunt.

SMUGGLING

By this time we had accumulated a full wagon load of clothes and medicine, the latter mostly quinine. The question now was how to get it to our army. Luckily, I still had an abundance of greenbacks and succeeded, by the offer of an exorbitant amount, in hiring a German with his wagon and team to haul the goods to our line. We had learned that there was a force of Confederate Cavalry thirty miles south of Memphis. With the goods safely loaded, the German and I started over the rough untraveled roads, practically trails, avoiding the highway, making very slow progress until brought to a complete halt by a stream swollen very much by recent rains. The ford on the main road was guarded, and the German rebelled, declaring he would go no further. I unhitched one of the horses, knowing he could not get away with but one, and mounting the horse entered the river. We swam from one side to the other, searching the banks for a possible crossing point, which I did not locate until we had crossed and recrossed many times. Having discovered a spot where I thought we might cross in safely, I returned to the German who flatly refused to make the attempt, so I was obliged to force him to drive at the point of my pistol. We reached the opposite bank without mishap and made all the speed possible through the remainder of the night. Just after daylight we were overtaken by a company of Confederate cavalry who pulled both the German and me from our seats on the wagon, tied our hands behind us, and sent us, both mounted on the same horse, under guard forward to their command, where we were regarded as smugglers and placed in the "bull pen" with a number of other prisoners, team and wagon and its contents being confiscated. The following day I learned from a guard that a friend of both Brother Jim and myself, Colonel Basil Duke, was in command. I managed to send him a note, and it seemed but a moment before he had me by the hand listening to my story.[5] Without loss of time men were sent in every direction, and by morning all my goods were restored to me, but the wagon and team, the Colonel explained, he would be obliged to hold. Out of courtesy to myself, the German was given a pass though our lines, and I paid him all he asked in compensation for his loss. His demand was not modest, and being granted he went away contented. The next day I and my goods were safely conducted to the railroad miles distant, and there all my plunder was loaded in a box car, and I, in charge, started on that weary ride south to our army.

BACK TO THE ARMY

Finally my car reached Meridian, Mississippi, and was placed on a side track. I locked the car door and started off to find my command. It was after sunset before I located it. My regiment, the picket told me, was that group of tents on the hillside yonder. Oh! Could it be possible that that was all there was left of the nineteen hundred and sixty men whose names had been on its muster roll? I inquired for Company "E," of which my brother Jim was Captain. I found the tents all situated with their backs to a steep hill, into which they had excavated, making most commodious quarters, with fireplace and chimney. It happened that many of the regimental and company officers were spending the evening with Brother Jim, smoking and telling stories. I learned afterward that I had been the subject of their conversation. How plain is the picture of that scene, as I drew back the blanket that served as a door and stood in the opening. Instantly conversation ceased. A light fall of snow lay on the ground outside, and my eyes, partially dazzled by its whiteness, could not at once adjust themselves to the dim obscurity of the room. Finally I discerned through the clouds of smoke a group of men as at a command arose, then Brother Jim came into view, leaning against the rude fireplace, pipe in mouth. Now these were brave and tried soldiers every one, but no ghostly apparition ever struck such terror to the human heart as did my sudden and unlooked for presence as I stood in the opening quietly facing them. The pipe dropped from Brother Jim's lips, his face turned ashy white, and he would have fallen had a comrade not rushed forward and caught him. My sudden appearance had stricken them dumb, but when I finally spoke, and they realized I was flesh and blood, and not my own ghost, they gradually recovered. They had all believed me dead, as my absence had covered many months. Never before nor since did Brother Jim kiss me, but that night he folded me in his arms and kissed me as a mother would her child. There was no sleep for me that night, nor for many following nights, as the anxious inquiries had to be answered, although some of the messages I brought came too late, and the ears that were to have received them were deaf forever to human tongue. It was a sad return. Many of those dear comrades from whom I expected the warmest welcome were not there to greet me, and I should never see them more. The list of dead and wounded had grown very long during my absence, and the knowledge of their sufferings and privations filled my heart with sorrow, but in spite of all this, no note of discouragement was uttered. I had presents for all, cloth for suits, pocket knives, and trinkets. Many went to the new comrades who had taken the places of those who were gone.

"Fall in," rang out the bugle. The remnant of that once great army, in battle array, started on its last race with death, its ranks reduced over eighty per cent during the past year by the ravages of war. Physically unfit, yet still undaunted, undiscouraged, brave unto death.

General Lee had surrendered, but as yet we were unaware of this, and the rumors which floated through our command were to the effect that General Lee had won a great victory; that Major General Kirby Smith, with a large army, was making forced marches to get in the enemy's rear, and so we fought on. The long and weary marches through the day and nights of that last retreat are to me the most cruel pages of the history of our war. The enemy, like blood hounds, were ever at our throats, overwhelming us completely by the number of their forces. Curtis, some day, when you are older, you will hunt the deer, and the hounds will trail the wounded by their blood. So it was with us. In the wake of our army, not only was our trail marked with blood of the dead and wounded, but by the bodies of the sick and exhausted men who could withstand no longer and so fell by the wayside. We kept only our guns and ammunition, and were compelled to abandon all baggage and commissary wagons. Still we fought on. We were told that Major General Kirby Smith would on the morrow get in the enemy's rear and so capture the entire army, and the next day it would still be "tomorrow," but that "tomorrow" never came. They had killed the horses and captured our artillery with the exception of six guns. Then the third day before the last, a large force suddenly charged our weakened left flank, killed the remaining horses and gunners, and took from us those guns, but not for long. You cannot realize, nor can I picture to you the diabolical frenzy of man when driven to desperation. We were starving, exhausted, haunted, sick, and the future was a blank, holding out no promise to us. We had been hounded and driven until death lost its terrors and rather stood to us for rest from all this strife and bloodshed.

A shout filled the air, not the famous rebel yell that is mentioned in all history, but one that seemingly came from the throats of demons in their last death struggle. It was so sudden, so appalling, so desperate, it struck terror to the Federals, and like maniacs, we were at their throats in hand to hand conflict. We succeeded in driving them back and recaptured our beloved guns.

Those tired, sick, and barefoot men pulled the guns by means of ropes through the twelve miles, ankle deep in bog and mire, until we came to some old breastworks General Beauregard had built during the early years of the war.

THE LAST BATTLE

Now, here is a picture which can be erased only by death. The exact location I do not know, but on a hill to our right the enemy had planted a battery and the next morning began to pour grape shot into our thin ranks while solid lines advanced in our front. We repulsed them, at nine o'clock the battery on the hill ceased firing and there ensued a calm. The men looked into each others faces with wonder and amazement. One man said, "Boys, Kirby Smith has gotten in their rear, and they are in full retreat." All that afternoon not a shot was fired, and how long that night seemed to those men watchful and sleepless. The only sound to be heard was the steady tramp of the sentinel. We could sleep under the roar of artillery and rattle of musketry, but what meant this deathly stillness? Unconsciously the men spoke in whispers, and the question that passed from lip to lip was, "What does it mean?"

The stillness was yet unexplained when the next morning some one mentioned he had not seen "Big officer" lately. Just then we saw our gallant Colonel riding toward us on his emaciated horse, and a moment later the bugle rang out the command to fall in.

THE SURRENDER

It seems to be pitiful to write that on that day those of our regiment answering for duty numbered much less than a company. "Color bearers ten paces to the front. About face." Those were the Colonel's orders, and his next "Present Arms." Stopping a moment he looked at us and then slowly turned and rode down the hill. "Look at the colonel, he's drunk. See, he can't keep his saddle," said the men. The Colonel checked his horse at some distance and beckoned the bugler to approach. A moment later the boy came running back, and with tears streaming down his face, said, "Boys, the Colonel says its all over. You will have to ground arms."

No tongue or pen can ever describe this scene. Our eyes involuntarily turned in the direction of that beloved battle flag which had never known dishonor or disgrace, and we thought of the many, many heroes who had died under it, and with one accord we struggled to obtain a scrap of it. I cannot write more.

The war was over, and we had lost. God only knows the price we paid.[6]

TRANSPORTATION

We were paroled and sent to the Mississippi River and promised transportation to St. Louis. The war at a close, and the necessity that had kept us blind to our own condition removed, our neglected bodies suffered an almost total collapse. Physically, we were in a worse condition than when we surrendered at Vicksburg and much more exhausted from the strenuous marching, to which was added the disease that was rife among us. Our clothing would scarcely cover our bodies, and we were, almost without exception, shoeless.

Without regard to commands we were loaded on every passing steamboat in much the same manner that cattle are loaded in a box car, and on the little steamboat on which I was packed there was not room for the men to lie down, while at almost every step some poor, sick fellow was shoved from the gang plank. The crew was composed of men too cowardly to fight with the army but brave enough, now that the war was over, to curse and abuse us. My exhaustion became so great that I could stand upright no longer. The boat was landing at Helena, Arkansas, when the mate spied me lying on the deck—he ordered two brutal negro deck hands to carry me off, and the boat pulled off, leaving me lying there on the levee bank. A negro woman found me and took me to her cabin. Poor woman, she had nothing but corn cake and dried pumpkin, but she gave me freely of it and would go with me, when I became able to walk, to the landing place and, as boats landed, would plead with them to take me aboard, only to be refused. I had no money and no hope.

HOMECOMING

After weeks of her motherly nursing I felt much better, and one day told her I was going to walk to Missouri. "No, honey, don't try it. You will sure die if you do," was her advice. However, with a big hoe cake, the only provision she had made for me, I started on that long, weary tramp over a country that had been ravished by both armies and in which not a building or so much as a fence or head of stock remained. During the ninety miles I covered I did not see a white person. It seemed as if some terrible scourge had destroyed every living thing. I met several parties of negroes, some hunting their former master or mistress, and others going North for that "mule and forty acres." Without exception they shared their scant provisions with me, and one very kindly tied up my sore feet, as only a darkie knows how. I must have been a pitiful sight, for I won the sympathy of all I met. At last, I came to a wide, seemingly endless prairie. How hot the sun was, and how hard it was to drag my poor, sore feet and weary legs over that rough and overgrown road. It was more than twenty-four hours since the last bit of my hoe cake had been eaten, and sick, discouraged, and exhausted, I dropped on the grass, and feeling myself now thoroughly beaten. I prayed that I might die. Nothing seemed to matter to me now but to be at peace.

THE LIGHT

I must have lain there hours, for when I partly aroused myself it was dark, then I saw to my great amazement and surprise, in the timber to my left, a light. It was the first indication of life or habitation that had crossed my vision in that long and weary struggle I had made against exhaustion and death. I lay there pondering—somehow it seemed the light said "come on," but my poor weakened body refused to obey my mind's command. The dew had fallen, and the chill of the night air had so encompassed me that I was only able to get on my hands and feet—to in a moment fall. It seemed someone said—"What's the use, by morning you will be at peace"—but more persistent came a pleading voice, "Come on, come on." The light seemed to haunt me, and I resolved to make one more effort. The light seemed to keep saying "Come on." I reached the clearing and saw two log cabins with a passageway between. There was no fence or outbuildings. The passageway was raised. I was just about to knock when the sound of voices reached my ears, and I realized that family prayer was being held within. I heard the voice of an old man praying for Dick, Jim, and Little Johnnie, and then I recognized my father's voice. It seemed the most natural thing in the world to me, as I rested against the side of the wall, fascinated by the latch on the door and wondering in a vague sort of way why they put it on the outside of the door. It never occurred to me to interrupt the prayer, but I mentally wondered if he would ever cease. My sensibilities were numbed, and nothing seemed unusual. I never questioned as to why he was here in this log cabin in such a God forsaken country. At last came the "Amen," and I knocked. A woman's voice said, "Come in," and I opened the door. There was a fire on the hearth where they had cooked their evening meal. On a shelf on the wall a candle was burning. And there, all three standing, were my old Father, sister Sarah, and Mary, brother Dick's wife. Instinctively I had known who would be there before I opened the door. They stared at me with wondering eyes. Something held us all speechless. I was groping blindly in my mind for words. Finally they came—"I've come home," I said and collapsed. Sister Sarah caught my tottering body and helped me to a bench. "Something to eat," I managed to say. Sister Mary ran to start the fire and put the bacon in the skillet and the rye in the coffee pot. My old Father supported me while Sarah brought me a drink. They knew I had been a Confederate soldier, although none recognized me. It was no wonder, for since leaving Memphis nearly a year ago, I had scarcely seen a piece of soap. I was now almost nineteen years of age with only sufficient flesh to cover my bones. "To what command did you belong," asked my Father, but to all his questions I could only shake my head. The frying pan had all my attention. Thank God, Mary was placing it on the table, and Father and Sarah were taking me to the bench in front of it. My boy, I was as unaccustomed to eat with a knife or fork as you are accustomed to their use. When they placed me at the table I seized the bacon in both my hands and devoured it like an animal. Mary was at the other side of the table with her chin resting on her hands watching me, when suddenly she gave a scream and cried, "It is Jim." (Jim was my next oldest brother.) They gathered around me, embracing me between their tears, and when I could sufficiently control my voice, I told that I was Johnnie. My Father brought the water, and they all helped to bathe me. My sisters that night made me underclothes from their skirts. Weeks after, I learned that Father and my Sisters, knowing that the war was over and unable to wait longer for news of us, had started South with a pair of horses and carryall, or light spring wagon, loaded with provisions and supplies. On reaching that lonely place, robbers had captured the horses, wagon, and all they had brought and had left them stranded in that little cabin.[7]

Notes
Bibliography
Index

Notes

1. In his 2002 work *Still Fighting the Civil War: The American South and Southern History* (Baton Rouge: Louisiana State University Press, 2002), David Goldfield tells of another Southern memoir in which fiction overwhelmed fact. James Avirett's 1901 memoir, *The Old Plantation: How We Lived in Great House and Cabin Before the War,* is almost entirely fabricated, reflecting more the image of the South after the Civil War than Avirett's own life. Still Goldfield urges that it not be dismissed out of hand but considered part of the discussion of how Southerners viewed themselves in the years after the war. The memoir is discussed on page 21 of the work.

2. For extensive discussion of the Lost Cause and related Southern myths, see Gaines M. Foster, *Ghosts of the Confederacy: Defeat, the Lost Cause, and the Emergence of the New South, 1865–1913* (New York: Oxford University Press, 1987); Rollin G. Osterweis, *The Myth of the Lost Cause, 1865–1900* (Hamden, CT: Archon Books, 1973); E. A. Pollard, *The Lost Cause: The Standard Southern History of the War of the Confederates* (New York: E. B. Treat, 1867; repr., New York: Bonanza Books, 1974); and Gary W. Gallagher and Alan T. Nolan, eds., *The Myth of the Lost Cause and Civil War History* (Bloomington: Indiana University Press, 2000).

3. C. Vann Woodward, *Origins of the New South, 1877–1913.* (Baton Rouge: Louisiana State University Press, 1951), 156. Osterweis, *Myth of Lost Cause,* 93.

4. Cox, *Dixie's Daughters,* 15–16, 75, 84.

5. The 1890 figures are from the 1890 census. The 1900 and 1910 estimates are based on survival rates from John Ruoff's "Southern Womanhood, 1865–1920: An Intellectual and Cultural Study" (Ph.D. diss., University of Illinois at Urbana-Champaign, 1976), 98. Ruoff estimates that 81 percent of veterans alive in 1880 were alive in 1900. However, only 36 percent of those alive in 1880 were living in 1910. The figures for 1922 are from United Daughters of the Confederacy surveys contained in R. B. Rosenburg, *Living Monuments: Confederate Soldiers' Homes in the New South* (Chapel Hill: University of North Carolina Press, 1993), 163–64.

6. Frances Gleason's history of Laclede County, Missouri, describes Isaac's arrival as "important" and his home as "almost palatial." The Wickershams figure prominently in her work for the entire Civil War era; Gleason, *First Hundred Years,* 20–30. *The History of Laclede County, Missouri* also includes a section on the Wickershams and describes their arrival in the area. Richard had married Mary Weigle in the mid 1850s. Biographical information on the Wickersham family is from census records, county histories, and discussions with Becky Pierce. Johnnie never officially enlisted in the Confederate military, and a search of service records provided by Broadfoot Publishing revealed no official mention of him, although both his older brothers are documented.

7. Peterson et al., *Sterling Price's Lieutenants,* 205. The unit was formed in the fall of 1861. The Seventh Division of the State Guard included men from eighteen counties (including Laclede) in south central Missouri. The Missouri State Guard was organized geographically (22–24). Military information about Richard and James is from their compiled service records, the supplemental volumes of the *War of the Rebellion* (hereafter cited as *The Official Records*) and Richard's obituary in the *Lebanon Rustic.* James lived in Arkansas for a short period after the war and then returned to Lebanon. He died in Missouri in 1892.

8. Price's 1864 raid into Missouri was his attempt to reclaim the state for the South. The raid was a failure, and of the twelve thousand men who started the journey, only six thousand were left when Price retreated from the state for the final time.

Richard moved to Arkansas for a short period after the war and returned to Lebanon in 1869. He served as postmaster for the city and was mayor for a short time. Richard was the last surviving Wickersham son, surviving until 1917; Gleason, *First Hundred Years,* 763–64.

9. Although this move was prompted by Curtis's job, the Wickersham and Wright families were not alone in moving from the South to California. Nina Silber, in *The Romance of Reunion: Northerners and the South, 1865–1900* (Chapel Hill: University of North Carolina Press, 1993), indicates "plenty of Southerners" made the move west (190).

10. David Blight, *Race and Reunion: The Civil War in American Memory* (Cambridge, MA: Belknap Press, 2001), 8. Goldfield's *Still Fighting the Civil War* also discusses the ways in which memories of the war changed over time, even for its participants.

1. "MEMORY SEEMS SO REAL"

1. Franz Sigel (Wickersham's "General Seigel") was a German immigrant popular with the many German Union soldiers in St. Louis. He participated in the battle of Wilson's Creek and remained in the Union Army until May 1865. He was most noted for his ability to recruit German immigrants for the Union cause. Boatner, *Civil War Dictionary,* 761.

2. Wickersham is quoting from "Root, Abe, or Die," a song sung to the tune of "Root, Hog, or Die." The song starts with the lines

The Dutch came to Missouri, as well you all do know,
To subjugate the rebel boys but couldn't make it go.
They can't whip the rebel boys, and I'll tell you the reason
  why,
The Southern boys made them run—Root hog or die.

3. General Nathaniel Lyon was killed attempting to rally his troops at the battle of Wilson's Creek on August 10, 1861. Wilson's Creek was a Confederate victory, and Union forces were forced to retreat back to Springfield.

4. Joe Crawford is probably Joe Craig. Peterson et al., *Sterling Price's Lieutenants,* names Joe (or Joel, both spellings being given in his service record) Craig as the other lieutenant for this company. These were the officers for the Laclede County Company of the Third Infantry Regiment of the Seventh Division of the Missouri State Guard. The division was commanded by Brigadier General James Haggin McBride. Major General Sterling Price was the overall commander of the Patriot Army of Missouri.

5. The Maynard carbine was a common Civil War weapon. It weighed about six pounds and was just over three feet long.

6. This is the Laclede (Lebanon) Company of the Third Infantry Regiment of the Seventh Division of the Missouri State Guards.

7. Major Frank White was captured by Missouri state troops approximately the same time as Zagonyi's Charge and freed shortly after the battle.

8. Fremont's Body Guards were an elite unit, at least in the eyes of John Fremont. They are described as wearing "blue jackets, trousers, and caps" and being armed with German sabers and "mounted upon bay horses." "Fremont's Hundred Days," 251. The unit was disbanded shortly after this engagement.

9. Schnetzer's *More Forgotten Men* lists a Charles C. McCall from Lebanon as being engaged at this battle. There is no confirmation of his death available, although at least one hundred Confederate soldiers were killed (152).

10. Wickersham is describing Zagonyi's Charge (October 25, 1861) here. Major Charles Zagonyi of Fremont's Body Guards led his force on a charge just outside Springfield, sending the Confederate forces fleeing. There is disagreement as to which Union soldier was killed by Wickersham. Switzler's *History of Missouri* reports that he killed Lieutenant Patrick Connolly. Holcombe's

History of Greene County, Missouri says it was Corporal Norrison or Norton, not Connolly. A 2004 *North and South* article by Kip Lindberg and Jeff Patrick accepts Wickersham's version completely, and the authors believe he killed Connolly. Zagonyi's report lists "Lt. Conolly" among the fatalities, along with six unnamed corporals. He also reported that at least 106 Confederates were killed. An anonymous comrade in 1886 supports Wickersham's story of his action, including his swearing, in the *Missouri Republican.*

11. Without further description it is hard to determine exactly to which revolver Wickersham is referring. Colt made the most common dragoon revolvers used in the war, and silver plating was not uncommon.

12. State records do not show any pardon of a Joe Craig or Joe Crawford for murder between 1865 and 1900.

13. Probably this is Dr. John Henry Britts of Henry County, Missouri. Britts was a prominent surgeon who served with the Confederate military for the entire war despite being severely wounded during the siege of Vicksburg.

2. "THE FIRST TIME I HEARD 'DIXIE'"

1. Thomas Lowndes Snead was a journalist who became chief of staff for both Governor Jackson and General Price. He was a Confederate congressman and wrote his account of the Missouri battles in "The First Year of the War in Missouri."

2. Colton Greene was Fourth Commander of the Seventh Division of the State Guard when it was formed and was promoted to colonel after the battle of Elkhorn Tavern. He took over the Third Missouri Regiment of the regular Confederate Army shortly thereafter and commanded that regiment for the rest of the war. After the war he fled to Mexico briefly before returning to spend the rest of his life in Memphis, where he died in 1900. Allardice, "Colonel Colton Greene."

3. The two Missouri regiments paraded through Springfield on January 1, 1862. Bevier, *History,* 86.

4. The army arrived at Cassville, Missouri, on February 15, 1862.

5. There were approximately 12,100 Union soldiers in Lebanon during January and February of 1862.

6. Wickersham is probably referring to his brother Dick here, not anyone named Bill.

7. Mary Wickersham was about twenty-five years old at this time and had two young daughters. She was the daughter of Prussian immigrants.

8. Lizzie Harrison was born about 1848. The 1870 census shows her married to Dr. Robert W. Fyan, a lawyer and judge in Marshfield, Missouri, and the mother of a two-year-old son and one-month-old daughter.

9. Sarah Gibbs was Johnnie's oldest sibling. She was fourteen years older than Johnnie and was married to Will Gibbs.

10. Dudley Wickersham was a colonel in the Tenth Illinois Cavalry Regiment. This regiment spent most of the war in Missouri, Arkansas, Mississippi, and Louisiana. Wickersham survived the war and died in 1898 in Illinois.

11. Price was headquartered at Neosho during the fall of 1861. He moved into winter quarters outside Osceola after that. Both of those locations are approximately seventy miles from Springfield. Snead, "First Year," 274.

12. Wickersham is probably referring to Captain Richmond Hobson, who gained fame during the Spanish-American War when he attempted to block Santiago de Cuba harbor by sinking his ship in its entrance.

13. The story of Johnnie being kissed while riding with Price is also told by "One of Them" in the *Missouri Republican* on December 8, 1886.

14. The *Missouri Army Argus* of January 23, 1862, included a call for "boys of John Wickersham's pluck" to join his new company by reporting to the adjutant general of Brigadier General McBride's division.

15. General James Haggin McBride was first appointed brigadier general of the Seventh Division of the Missouri State Guards. He resigned on February 23, 1862, after falling out of favor with

Price. He raised two regiments from Arkansas for the Confederate army but fell ill and was unable to fight with them. He died in 1864 of pneumonia. Allardice, *More Generals in Gray,* 144–56.

16. There is no record of a Confederate General Hale from West Point. Stephen F. Hale commanded the Fourth Infantry Regiment of the Eighth Division of the State Guards. He reportedly resigned January 4, 1862, but also was reported wounded in the spring of 1862. Peterson et al., *Sterling Price's Lieutenants,* 232; Bartels, *Forgotten Men,* 141.

17. James was a first lieutenant in Company E of the Fourth Missouri Infantry.

18. General James McIntosh died at Pea Ridge and was the brother of Union general John McIntosh. The Indians mentioned by Wickersham were three regiments commanded by Albert Pike. The only major action of the war they would see was at Pea Ridge.

19. Van Dorn was given command of the Trans-Mississippi District on January 10, 1862. This was part of General A. S. Johnston's Confederate Department No. 2, which included a huge amount of territory from the Appalachians to Indian Territory. Earl Van Dorn was from Mississippi. He was a graduate of West Point and a veteran of the Mexican War. As commander of the Trans-Mississippi Department of the Confederate Army, he was a failure, losing both his major battles at Pea Ridge and Corinth. Van Dorn was murdered in 1863 by an irate husband. Faust, *Historical Times,* 777–78.

20. The battle of Pea Ridge occurred March 7–8, 1862. The Confederate forces were defeated and driven back to the Mississippi River. Approximately twenty-five thousand total troops engaged in this battle, which resulted in about twenty-one hundred casualties. See Shea and Hess's *Pea Ridge* for a complete account of the battle.

21. Generals Ben McCulloch of Texas and James McIntosh of the Second Arkansas were killed, and Colonel Louis Hebert was captured at Pea Ridge.

22. No firm estimates on the casualty figures exist for McDonald's unit. However, Shea and Hess, in *Pea Ridge,* do discuss the numerous close calls that the battery had during the battle and their narrow escape from the field.

23. Measles was an especially common problem among new Civil War recruits. Bollet estimates more than seventy-six thousand cases among Union soldiers. The Confederate Army was hit worse. The Twelfth North Carolina saw eight hundred of its twelve hundred recruits hit with the disease. Measles was much more common early in the war than late. Bollet, *Civil War Medicine,* 269–71.

3. "WE FOUGHT EACH OTHER LIKE WILD ANIMALS"

1. On March 17, 1862, the state guard units were transferred to the Confederate Army.

2. Wickersham's description of the weapons is relatively accurate. Flintlocks are weapons dating from the American Revolution. The best infantrymen could fire them two or three times a minute, and they were accurate up to about thirty yards.

3. Colonel John Quincy Burbridge was a Missouri businessman and the commander of the First Missouri Confederate Infantry Regiment. Burbridge was wounded at Pea Ridge and left the unit. He did not leave the war effort, instead leading guerrilla raids back into Missouri, such as the one Wickersham describes. Tucker, *South's Finest,* 1.

4. Most Missouri units (including the First) arrived at Shiloh immediately after the major battle there. Tucker, *South's Finest,* 44. There is confusion over whether these forces actually made it to Shiloh. Robert Hartje's 1967 biography of Van Dorn states that the general and his men never made it, instead arriving in Memphis on April 13, having been slowed on their march through Arkansas by flooding and mud (167–68). Wickersham is mistaken in identifying Joseph Johnston as the commander at Shiloh. Albert Sidney Johnston was in command of Confederate Depart-

ment No. 2 (which included all of Tennessee) until his death at the battle of Shiloh. P. G. T. Beauregard took command after Johnston's death. Faust, *Historical Times,* 216.

5. Van Dorn and Price's troops attacked the heavily fortified Union lines at Corinth, Mississippi, on October 3, 1862. The Confederate artillery was overwhelmed by Union artillery, and the Confederates were forced to retreat on October 4. There were more than five thousand total casualties in the two-day battle. See Cozzens, *Darkest Days,* for a detailed account of the battles of Corinth and Iuka.

6. Both sides used Parrott guns, which were rifled, muzzle-loaded canon. A thirty-pound Parrott gun had a maximal range of forty-four hundred yards. Boatner, *Civil War Dictionary,* 621.

7. From Wickersham's description it is impossible to precisely locate this plantation or to identify its owner. It seems most likely to have been between Vicksburg and Memphis, with northern Mississippi being most probable.

8. Colonel Emmett McDonald of the Second Missouri Cavalry was killed in Hartville, Missouri, on January 23, 1864. His death was the result of being shot in the left thigh. Anders, *Confederate Roll,* 87.

9. The battle of Big Black River Bridge, Mississippi, occurred on May 17, 1863. General Martin Green's Confederate troops of Missouri and Arkansas soldiers burned the bridge across the Big Black River to prevent Union troops from pursuing. The Confederate troops fled across the burning bridge and into Vicksburg. Faust, *Historical Times,* 59–60.

4. "I WALKED WITH MILITARY BEARING"

1. The units were at Demopolis during July and August of 1863. *Official Records* supplement vol. 38, part 2, serial 50, 394.

2. Brigadier General Matthew Ector commanded the Fourteenth Texas Infantry at Vicksburg. Ector was wounded during the Atlanta campaign and returned to service just before the surrender. He died in 1879, a judge on the Texas Court of Appeals.

3. Dalton, Georgia, saw battles throughout 1864, the major action occurring February 22–27, 1864.

4. Wickersham is listing a series of battles that were all part of the Atlanta campaign and occurred during the summer of 1864.

5. The battle of Kennesaw Mountain occurred on June 27, 1864. The Confederates repulsed numerous Union assaults, killed Brigadier General Charles G. Harker and Colonel Daniel Mc-Cook, and inflicted more than three thousand casualties on the federal troops. The Rebels lost about 750 men. Faust, *Historical Times,* 413.

6. Hiram Bledsoe was a native of Kentucky and a Mexican War veteran who reached the rank of colonel in the Confederate Army. After the war, Bledsoe served in the Missouri state senate. He died in 1906.

7. The battle of Franklin, Tennessee, occurred on November 30, 1864. General Hood was pursuing Union general Schofield, whose men dug earthworks and awaited the Confederates. Hood ordered a direct assault on the entrenched men, and the result of the day's battle was a disaster for the Confederates. Hood lost more than six thousand men, while the Union lost just over twenty-three hundred. Faust, *Historical Times,* 284–85. The Missouri Brigade was decimated during the charge, at one point receiving fire from three sides. The brigade suffered a 62 percent casualty rate at Franklin. Tucker, "First Missouri Brigade," 30. Johnnie apparently missed this battle, but James was there.

8. *Chevaux-de-frise* refers to any defensive obstacle topped with some kind of spike that is designed to stop a direct, frontal assault.

9. John Bell Hood replaced Johnston on July 17, 1864.

10. Wickersham is mistaken in the date here. The action he describes (including the death of General McPherson) occurred on July 22, 1864. On that day Hood attempted to attack McPherson's forces outside Atlanta. The assault was temporarily effective, but Union reinforcements stopped the Confederate advance. Hood lost more than eight thousand men, while the Union lost about thirty-seven hundred. After this it was only a matter of

time before Sherman was able to move in and capture Atlanta in September. Faust, *Historical Times,* 27–30.

11. Without knowing which state Hadley was from, it is impossible to further identify him. There is no mention of any Hadley in the *Official Records* of the campaign or in the prisoner-of-war reports in the *Official Records.* A search by Broadfoot Publishing found three records of a Richard Hadley, none of whom match Wickersam's description. The National Park Service Soldiers and Sailors System shows 520 Hadleys in the Union Army.

5. "TO SURRENDER WE KNEW MEANT DEATH"

1. James Wickersham's service records show him as being absent from the First and Fourth Missouri during at least August and September of 1864. He was assigned to Colonel James D. Hill's Scouts by order of General Hood. There is almost no discussion of the activities of this group outside the mention in the *Official Records* discussed below.

2. Hill was the aide-de-camp for General Hood during this time. Crute, *Confederate Staff,* 91.

3. Acworth is about thirty miles north of Atlanta, near Kennesaw, and was a station on the Western and Atlantic Railroad.

4. Because there are no records available on this group of men, identifying the individuals named by Wickersham throughout this section is extremely difficult.

5. Mt. Tamalpais is a twenty-five-hundred-foot hill about seventeen miles northwest of San Francisco.

6. Most likely this is U.S. senator Ben Tillman of South Carolina. Tillman gave a number of speeches on the "true" nature of African Americans, but his most famous was "The Race Problem," given to the Senate on February 23 and 24, 1903. During that oration, Tillman discussed at length the inability of African Americans to elevate themselves, through suffrage and education, beyond their nature.

7. Major General Joseph Wheeler commanded the cavalry of the Army of Tennessee. He led a number of raids against communication and railroad lines in 1863 and 1864. Boatner, *Civil*

War Dictionary, 910. Wheeler's October 9, 1864, official report indicates he left a detachment of two hundred men in North Georgia to destroy selected railroad lines at "five or six designated points." *Official Records* 38 series 1, part 3, 958. The report does not specify the units involved, nor is there any follow-up in the *Official Records.* The *Daily Intelligencer* of Macon, Georgia, kept track of Wheeler's cavalry and noted on August 31, 1864, that it was ten days since word had been heard from his "well-mounted" force ordered to attack the enemy's rear. However, by September 10 the same newspaper called Wheeler's raid a failure and called for Nathaniel Forrest's cavalry to be brought in.

8. Sherman's troops were equally adept at repairing and destroying railroads.

6. "THEY STARED AT ME WITH WONDERING EYES"

1. The steamship *Sultana* made regular trips between St. Louis and New Orleans throughout 1864. This is the same ship that sank in April 1865 after the boilers exploded. More than seventeen hundred passengers died, many of them former Union prisoners who were finally on their way home from the war. See Salecker, *Disaster on the Mississippi,* for a full description of the creation and destruction of the *Sultana.*

2. None of the available sources list a Henry Ashbrook from Missouri as being killed at Vicksburg. The closest match is a Private C. P. Ashworth who died at Little Rock, Arkansas, on June 30, 1863. Anders, *Confederate Roll,* 5.

3. Hawkins Wickersham was a merchant in St. Louis. He died in St. Louis on September 9, 1888, at the age of eighty-four. Hawkins was married to Sarah, meaning it was probably Aunt Sarah, not an Aunt Mary, to whom Johnnie is referring in this section.

4. It was most likely not Barnum's Circus in Missouri at this time. Frank J. Howes' circus toured Missouri during the Civil War and is probably the one Wickersham saw. Chindahl, *History of the Circus,* 84–86. John H. Glenroy was a bareback rider for

Howes' circus and reports they were touring Missouri throughout the Fall of 1864. The company consisted of approximately fourteen performers, including two African Americans. There were acrobats, clowns, and contortionists in addition to Glenroy. Glenroy, *Ins and Outs,* 140.

5. Wickersham is probably mistaken about meeting Colonel Basil Duke here. Duke had taken command of Morgan's Cavalry in September 1864 and spent the rest of the war in eastern Kentucky and western Virginia. Duke was in Missouri when the Civil War began, and it is entirely likely that the Wickersham family was acquainted with him before the war. Duke, *Civil War Reminiscences.*

6. The Department of Trans-Mississippi under General Kirby Smith formally surrendered in New Orleans on May 26, 1865. Smith was not there at the time. He was in Texas trying to rally more troops. He returned to New Orleans to find he had no more troops there. Under most of the war's terms of surrenders, the Confederate soldiers were allowed to return home, after promising to not again take up arms. Faust, *Historical Times,* 735–37.

7. Wickersham's memoir ends suddenly with little explanation of how he met up with his family or what happened next. The overwhelming majority of Confederate soldiers merely walked home, depending on the kindness of civilians to provide them with food and shelter. Once home, they attempted to resume their lives.

Bibliography

Adamson, Hans Christian. *Rebellion in Missouri, 1861: Nathaniel Lyon and His Army of the West. The Rise of Brigadier General Nathaniel Lyon, USA, Who Saved Missouri from Secession in the Civil War.* Philadelphia: Chilton, 1961.

Allardice, Bruce. "Colonel Colton Greene: 'A Gallant and Conspicuous Figure.'" Sterling Price Camp No. 145. http://www.sterlingprice145.org/greene.htm. December 1, 2003.

———. *More Generals in Gray.* Baton Rouge: Louisiana State University Press, 1995.

Anders, Leslie, ed. and comp. *Confederate Roll of Honor: Missouri.* Warrensburg: West Central Missouri Genealogical Society and Library, 1989.

Bailey, Anne J. *The Chessboard of War: Sherman and Hood in the Autumn Campaign of 1864.* Lincoln: University of Nebraska Press, 2000.

Barlow, William P. "Remembering the Missouri Campaign of 1861." *Civil War Regiments: A Journal of the American Civil War* 5, no. 4: 20–60.

Barr, Alwyn. "Confederate Artillery in the Trans-Mississippi." *Military Affairs* 27, no. 2 (Summer 1963): 77–83.

Bartels, Carolyn M. *The Forgotten Men: Missouri State Guard.* Shawnee Mission, KS: Two Trails, 1995.

———. *Missouri Confederate Surrender: Shreveport & New Orleans, May 1865.* Shawnee Mission, KS: Two Trails, 1991.

———. *Trans-Mississippi Men at War.* Vol. 1. Independence, MO: Two Trails, 1998.

Bevier, R. S. *History of the First and Second Missouri Confederate Brigades, 1861–1865.* St. Louis: Bryan, Brand, 1879.

Bircher, William. *A Drummer-Boy's Diary.* Newell L. Chester, editor. St. Cloud, MN: North Star, 1995.

Black, Robert C. "The Railroads of Georgia in the Confederate War Effort." *Journal of Southern History* 13, no. 4 (November 1947): 511–34.

Blight, David W. *Race and Reunion: The Civil War in American Memory.* Cambridge: Belknap Press of Harvard University Press, 2001.

Boatner, Mark M. III. *The Civil War Dictionary.* New York: David McKay, 1959.

Bollet, Alfred J. *Civil War Medicine: Challenges and Triumphs.* Tucson: Galen Press, 2002.

Botkin, B. A., ed. *A Civil War Treasury of Tales, Legends and Folklore.* New York: Random House, 1960.

Bowen, Don R. "Guerilla War in Western Missouri, 1862–1865: Historical Extensions of the Relative Deprivation Hypothesis." *Comparative Studies in Society of History* 19, no. 1 (January 1977): 30–51.

Brownless, Richard S. *Gray Ghosts of the Confederacy: Guerilla Warfare in the West, 1861–1865.* Baton Rouge: Louisiana State University Press, 1958.

Castel, Albert. *General Sterling Price and the Civil War in the West.* Baton Rouge: Louisiana State University Press, 1968.

Chindahl, George L. *A History of the Circus in America.* Caldwell, ID: Caxton, 1959.

Cox, Karen L. *Dixie's Daughters: The United Daughters of the Confederacy and the Preservation of Confederate Culture.* Gainesville: University Press of Florida, 2003.

Cozzens, Peter. *The Darkest Days of the War: The Battles of Iuka*

& Corinth. Chapel Hill: University of North Carolina Press, 1997.

Crute, Joseph H., Jr. *Confederate Staff Officers, 1861–1865.* Powhatan, VA: Derwent Books, 1982.

Duke, Basil W. *The Civil War Reminiscences of General Basil W. Duke, C.S.A.* New introduction by James A. Ramage. New York: Cooper Square, 2001.

Dwyer, Christopher S. "Raiding Strategy: As Applied by the Western Confederate Cavalry in the American Civil War." *Journal of Military History* 63, no. 2 (April 1999): 263–81.

Dyer, John P. *"Fightin' Joe' Wheeler.* Baton Rouge: Louisiana State University Press, 1941.

Dyer, J. P. "Some Aspects of Cavalry Operations in the Army of Tennessee." *Journal of Southern History* 8, no. 2 (May 1942): 210–25.

Eakin, Joanne Chiles. *Missouri Confederate Reports.* Independence, MO, 1995.

Elam, Mark. "The Road to Atlanta: The Role of Geography in Command and Decision Making During the Atlanta Campaign." Ph.D. diss. Florida State University, 1996.

Faust, Patricia L. *Historical Times Illustrated Encyclopedia of the Civil War.* New York: Harper, 1986.

Fellman, Michael. *Inside War: the Guerilla Conflict in Missouri During the American Civil War.* New York: Oxford University Press, 1989.

Ford, Harvey S. "Van Dorn and the Pea Ridge Campaign." *Journal of the American Military Institute* 3, no. 4 (Winter 1939): 222–36.

"Fremont's Hundred Days in Missouri." *Atlantic Monthly* 9, no. 52 (February 1862): 247–59.

Frost, Dan R. *Thinking Confederates: Academia and the Idea of Progress in the New South.* Knoxville: University of Tennessee Press, 2000.

Gleason, Frances Ethel. *The First Hundred Years: Lebanon, Missouri.* Lebanon, MO: Laclede County Centennial, 1949.

Glenroy, John H. *Ins and Outs of Circus Life, or Forty-Two Years Travel of John H. Glenroy, Bareback Rider, Through United States, Canada, South America and Cuba.* Compiled by Stephen Stanley Stanford. Boston: M. M. Wing, 1885.

Groom, Winston. *Shrouds of Glory from Atlanta to Nashville: The Last Great Campaign of the Civil War.* New York: Atlantic Monthly Press, 1995.

Harding, James. *Service with the Missouri State Guard: The Memoir of Brigadier General James Harding.* Edited by James E. McGhee. Springfield, MO: Oak Hills, 2000.

Hartje, Robert G. *Van Dorn: The Life and Times of a Confederate General.* Nashville: Vanderbilt University Press, 1967.

Hay, Thomas Robson. "Confederate Leadership at Vicksburg." *Mississippi Valley Historical Review* 11, no. 4 (March 1925): 543–60.

———. "The Davis-Hood-Johnston Controversy of 1864." *Mississippi Valley Historical Review* 11, no. 1 (June 1924): 54–84.

History of Laclede, Camden, Dallas, Webster, Wright, Texas, Pulaski, Phelps, and Dent Counties, Missouri. Indexed Edition. From the Earliest Time to the Present, Including a Department Devoted to the Preservation of Sundry Personal Business, Professional and Private Records; Besides a Valuable Fund of Notes, Original Observations, Etc. Etc. Illustrated. Chicago: Goodspeed, 1889; repr., Independence, MO: BNL Library Services, 1974.

History of Laclede County, Missouri, The. Tulsa, OK: Lois Roper Board and Heritage Publishing, 1979.

Holcombe, R. *History of Greene County, Missouri.* St. Louis: Western Historical, 1883.

Hood, John Bell. *Advance and Retreat: Personal Experiences in the United States and Confederate States Armies.* New Orleans: Published for the Hood Orphan Memorial Fund, 1880.

Keesee, Dennis M. *Too Young to Die: Boy Soldiers of the Union Army, 1861–1865.* Huntington, WV: Blue Acorn, 2001.

Lindberg, Kip, and Jeff Patrick. "In the Shadow of the Light: The Charge of Fremont's Body Guard." *North and South: The Magazine of Civil War Conflict* 7, no. 3 (2004): 56–72.

Linderman, Gerald. *Embattled Courage: The Experience of Combat in the American Civil War.* New York: Free Press, 1987.

Logue, Larry M. *To Appomattox and Beyond: The Civil War Soldier in War and Peace.* Chicago: Ivan R. Dee, 1996.

McDonough, James Lee, and Thomas L. Connelly. *Five Tragic Hours: The Battle of Franklin.* Knoxville: University of Tennessee Press, 1983.

McMurry, Richard M. *Atlanta, 1864: Last Chance of the Confederacy.* Lincoln: University of Nebraska Press, 2000.

McPherson, James M. *For Cause & Comrades: Why Men Fought in the Civil War.* New York: Oxford University Press, 1997.

Mitchell, Reid. *Civil War Soldiers: Their Expectations and Their Experiences.* New York: Touchstone, 1988.

Moore, Waldo W. "The Defense of Shreveport: The Confederacy's Last Redoubt." *Military Affairs* 17, no. 2 (Summer 1953): 72–82.

Parrish, William E. *Turbulent Partnership: Missouri and the Union 1861–1865.* With an introduction by Robert L. D. Davidson. Columbia: University of Missouri Press, 1963.

Peterson, Richard C., James E. McGhee, Kip A. Lindberg, and Keith I. Daleen. *Sterling Price's Lieutenants: A Guide to the Officers and Organizations of the Missouri State Guard, 1861–1865.* Shawnee Mission, KS: Two Trails, 1995.

Pettegrew, John. "'The Soldiers' Faith': Turn-of-the-Century Memory of the Civil War and the Emergence of Modern American Nationalism." *Journal of Contemporary History* 31, no. 1 (January 1996): 49–73.

Piston, William Garrett, and Richard W. Hatcher III. *Wilson's Creek: The Second Battle of the Civil War and the Men Who Fought it.* Chapel Hill: University of North Carolina Press, 2000.

Royster, Charles. *The Destructive War: William Tecumseh Sherman, Stonewall Jackson, and the Americans.* New York: Vintage Civil War Library, 1991.

Salecker, Gene Eric. *Disaster on the Mississippi: The* Sultana *Explosion, April 27, 1865.* Annapolis, MD: Naval Institute Press, 1996.

Saxon, A. H. *P. T. Barnum: The Legend and the Man.* New York: Columbia University Press, 1989.

Schnetzer, Wayne, comp. *More Forgotten Men: Missouri State Guard.* Independence, MO: Two Trails, 2003.

Schrantz, Ward L., comp. *Jasper County, Missouri, in the Civil War.* Carthage, MO: Carthage, 1923.

Shalhope, Robert E. *Sterling Price: Portrait of a Southerner.* Columbia: University of Missouri Press, 1971.

Shea, William L., and Earl J. Hess. *Pea Ridge: Civil War Campaign in the West.* Chapel Hill: University of North Carolina Press, 1992.

Sigel, Franz. "The Pea Ridge Campaign." In *Battles and Leaders of the Civil War.* Vol. 1, 314–34. H-Bar Enterprises, 1997. CD-ROM.

Silber, Nina. *The Romance of Reunion: Northerners and the South, 1865–1900.* Chapel Hill: University of North Carolina Press, 1993.

Snead, Thomas L. "The First Year of the War in Missouri." In *Battles and Leaders of the Civil War.* Vol. 1, 262–77. H-Bar Enterprises, 1997. CD-ROM.

Switzler's Illustrated History of Missouri, from 1541 to 1877. Edited and published by C. R. Barns. St. Louis, 1879.

Tucker, Phillip Thomas. "Cannons on Little Kennesaw: The Role of the First Missouri Confederate Artillery Battery." *Atlanta History* 33, no. 2 (1989): 36–45.

———. "The First Missouri Brigade at the Battle of Franklin." *Tennessee Historical Quarterly* 46, no. 1 (1987): 21–32.

———. "Revenge for Atlanta?: The First Missouri Confederate Brigade and the Capture of Jonesboro, Georgia, September 6, 1864." *Journal of Confederate History* 2, no. 1 (1989): 93–113.

———. *The South's Finest: The First Missouri Confederate Brigade from Pea Ridge to Vicksburg.* Shippensburg, PA: White Mane, 1993.

Vandiver, Frank E. "General Hood as Logistician." *Military Affairs* 16, no. 1 (Spring 1952): 1–11.

War of the Rebellion: A Compilation of the Official Records of the Union and Confederate Armies. 128 vols. Washington, DC, 1880–1901.

Webb, W. L. *Battles and Biographies of Missourians or the Civil War Period of Our State.* Kansas City, MO: Hudson-Kimberly, 1900.

Wiley, Bell I. *The Life of Johnny Reb: The Common Soldier of the Confederacy.* Essential Classics of the Civil War. New York: Book-of-the-Month Club, 1951, 1957.

Wright, Curtis. *Genealogical and Biographical Notices of Descendants of Sir John Wright of Kelvedon Hall, Essex, England in America. Thomas Write, of Wethersfield, Connecticut. DEA Samuel Wright, of Northampton, Massachusetts, 1610–1670, 1614–1665.* Carthage, MO, 1915.

Index

In cases where names or dates used by Johnnie Wickersham differ from official records, those of Wickersham are shown in parentheses. The initials "JW" refer to Johnnie Wickersham.

Kathleen Gorman is an associate professor of history at Minnesota State University, Mankato, where she teaches U.S. history with a focus on the Civil War. She has written on the Reconstruction Ku Klux Klan and Confederate pensions, has published in the *Georgia Historical Quarterly*, and has contributed to *Before the New Deal: Social Welfare in the South, 1830–1930*, edited by Elna C. Green.